D1081854

Biography Today

Profiles
of People
of Interest
to Young
Readers

Volume 12
Issue 3
September 2003

Cherie D. Abbey
Managing Editor

Kevin Hillstrom
Editor

615 Griswold Street
Detroit, Michigan 48226

Cherie D. Abbey, *Managing Editor*
Kevin Hillstrom, *Editor*

Sheila Fitzgerald, Laurie Hillstrom, Sarah Lorenz,
and Sue Ellen Thompson, *Staff Writers*

Barry Puckett, *Research Associate*

Allison A. Beckett and Linda Strand, *Research Assistants*

Omnigraphics, Inc.

* * *

Matthew P. Barbour, *Senior Vice President*
Kay Gill, *Vice President — Directories*
Kevin Hayes, *Operations Manager*
Leif Gruenberg, *Development Manager*
David P. Bianco, *Marketing Consultant*

* * *

Peter E. Ruffner, *Publisher*
Frederick G. Ruffner, Jr., *Chairman*

This book is printed on acid-free paper meeting the ANSI Z39.48 Standard. The infinity symbol that appears above indicates that the paper in this book meets that standard.

Printed in the United States

INDEXED IN
Children's Magazine Guide

Contents

Preface

Biography Today is a magazine designed and written for the young reader — ages 9 and above — and covers individuals that librarians and teachers tell us that young people want to know about most: entertainers, athletes, writers, illustrators, cartoonists, and political leaders.

The Plan of the Work

The publication was especially created to appeal to young readers in a format they can enjoy reading and readily understand. Each issue contains approximately 10 sketches arranged alphabetically. Each entry provides at least one picture of the individual profiled, and bold-faced rubrics lead the reader to information on birth, youth, early memories, education, first jobs, marriage and family, career highlights, memorable experiences, hobbies, and honors and awards. Each of the entries ends with a list of easily accessible sources designed to lead the student to further reading on the individual and a current address. Obituary entries are also included, written to provide a perspective on the individual's entire career. Obituaries are clearly marked in both the table of contents and at the beginning of the entry.

Biographies are prepared by Omnigraphics editors after extensive research, utilizing the most current materials available. Those sources that are generally available to students appear in the list of further reading at the end of the sketch.

Indexes

A new index now appears in all *Biography Today* publications. In an effort to make the index easier to use, we have combined the **Name** and **General Index** into one, called the **Cumulative Index**. This new index contains the names of all individuals who have appeared in *Biography Today* since the series began. The names appear in bold faced type, followed by the issue in which they appeared. The General Index also contains the occupations, nationalities, and ethnic and minority origins of individuals profiled. The General Index is cumulative, including references to all individuals who have appeared in the *Biography Today* General Series and the *Biography Today* Special Subject volumes since the series began in 1992.

In a further effort to consolidate and save space, the Birthday and Places of Birth Indexes will be appearing only in the September issue and in the Annual Cumulation.

Our Advisors

This series was reviewed by an Advisory Board comprised of librarians, children's literature specialists, and reading instructors to ensure that the concept of this publication — to provide a readable and accessible biographical magazine for young readers — was on target. They evaluated the title as it developed, and their suggestions have proved invaluable. Any errors, however, are ours alone. We'd like to list the Advisory Board members, and to thank them for their efforts.

Sandra Arden, *Retired*
Assistant Director
Troy Public Library, Troy, MI

Gail Beaver
University of Michigan School of Information
Ann Arbor, MI

Marilyn Bethel, *Retired*
Broward County Public Library System
Fort Lauderdale, FL

Nancy Bryant
Brookside School Library,
Cranbrook Educational Community
Bloomfield Hills, MI

Cindy Cares
Southfield Public Library
Southfield, MI

Linda Carpino
Detroit Public Library
Detroit, MI

Carol Doll
Wayne State University Library and Information Science Program
Detroit, MI

Helen Gregory
Grosse Pointe Public Library
Grosse Pointe, MI

Jane Klasing, *Retired*
School Board of Broward County
Fort Lauderdale, FL

Marlene Lee
Broward County Public Library System
Fort Lauderdale, FL

Sylvia Mavrogenes
Miami-Dade Public Library System
Miami, FL

Carole J. McCollough
Detroit, MI

Rosemary Orlando
St. Clair Shores Public Library
St. Clair Shores, MI

Renee Schwartz
Broward County Public Library System
Fort Lauderdale, FL

Lee Sprince
Broward West Regional Library
Fort Lauderdale, FL

Susan Stewart, *Retired*
Birney Middle School Reading Laboratory, Southfield, MI

Ethel Stoloff, *Retired*
Birney Middle School Library
Southfield, MI

Our Advisory Board stressed to us that we should not shy away from controversial or unconventional people in our profiles, and we have tried to follow their advice. The Advisory Board also mentioned that the sketches might be useful in reluctant reader and adult literacy programs, and we would value any comments librarians might have about the suitability of our magazine for those purposes.

Your Comments Are Welcome

Our goal is to be accurate and up-to-date, to give young readers information they can learn from and enjoy. Now we want to know what you think. Take a look at this issue of *Biography Today*, on approval. Write or call me with your comments. We want to provide an excellent source of biographical information for young people. Let us know how you think we're doing.

Cherie Abbey
Managing Editor, *Biography Today*
Omnigraphics, Inc.
615 Griswold Street
Detroit, MI 48226

editor@biographytoday.com
www.biographytoday.com

Congratulations!

Congratulations to the following individuals and libraries, who are receiving a free copy of *Biography Today*, Vol. 12, No. 3 for suggesting people who appear in this issue:

Ayanna Black, Southfield, MI
Crystal Brown, Wheatland, OK
Jasmine Dillard, Chicago, IL
Catherine Harris, Pleasant Ridge, MI
Helen Ideno, Chicago, IL
Miranda Louis, Cambridge, MA
Jasmine McKinney, Stockton, CA
Howard Norris, Toledo, OH
Erica Perez, Chicago, IL
Tiffany Robertson, Melbourne, FL
Kierra Robinson, Toledo, OH
Sherry Shaheen, Oregon, OH
Donna Szatko, Chicago, IL
Tina Watson, Philadelphia, PA
Hana Yoshimoto, San Rafael, CA

Olivia Bennett 1989-

American Artist Known for Her Floral Watercolor
Paintings
Raised $33,000 to Aid Afghan Children through Sales
of Her Painting "Let Freedom Bloom"

BIRTH

Olivia Bennett was born in Salt Lake City, Utah, on August 16,
1989. Her father, Matt, is a grocery company executive, and her

mother, Michele, is a homemaker. She has a younger brother, Michael, and a younger sister, Sarah. In 1999, the Bennett family moved to Southlake, Texas, a booming community northeast of Fort Worth.

YOUTH

The first indications of Olivia Bennett's artistic talent appeared when she was in kindergarten. While other children her age tried to master coloring inside the lines, she already showed advanced drawing abilities. It was also around this time that the young girl was diagnosed with leukemia—a type of cancer in which the bone marrow produces abnormal numbers of white blood cells. Doctors treated her disease with chemotherapy, which involved injecting her with toxic chemicals to kill the cancer. Chemotherapy often causes side effects, such as nausea, weakness, and hair loss.

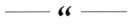

"I think I definitely appreciate life in a different way than I would if I hadn't had cancer," Bennett said.

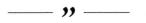

Bennett underwent chemotherapy for two years. Her mother recalled that the treatments made her very sick: "She was just out, on the couch violently ill." To make matters worse, one medication caused temporary nerve damage that made her hands curl up and become stiff, like claws. "I couldn't even hold a pencil," Bennett remembered. As she recovered from leukemia and chemotherapy, she turned to painting to occupy her time. She eventually overcame the disease and has been in remission (cancer-free) for several years. "I think I definitely appreciate life in a different way than I would if I hadn't had cancer," she stated.

Meanwhile, Bennett's artistic talent attracted considerable attention. When she was in third grade, she won first place in the Utah division of a national competition to design a postage stamp featuring a duck. Her winning painting was eventually turned into a stamp. She sold her first painting at the age of eight, when a visitor noticed it hanging on the wall in her home and insisted on giving her $50 for it. By the time Bennett was 11, a Fort Worth art gallery had asked to exhibit her work and represent her. "I think there is a reason why she is here [on earth]," her mother noted. "She went through so much and then to come out and have this gift . . . it's amazing."

*Many of Bennett's watercolor compositions are of flowers.
"Roses and magnolias are my favorites," she says.*

EDUCATION

Bennett attended Rockenbaugh Elementary in Southlake. A middle school student, she currently attends Eubanks Intermediate School in Southlake, where she is a straight-A student. "School is always my first priority, so homework comes before anything else," she explained.

Olivia Bennett's painting "Let Freedom Bloom"
raised $33,000 to aid Afghan children.

MAJOR ACCOMPLISHMENT

Despite her young age, Olivia's work has attracted the attention of art lovers across the country. Many people are drawn to the youthful energy in her paintings. In addition, some people find her work to be inspirational and feel that her paintings reflect her triumph over leukemia.

Olivia is best known for her large, vibrant watercolor paintings of flowers. "I don't know why [I paint] flowers," she noted. "I've just always been drawn towards them. Roses and magnolias are my favorites." She often visits flower gardens and takes pictures of the colorful blooms. "Mostly, I paint them from pictures, but when I do paint them live, I try to examine them and look at them, see how they grow," she explained. Her floral paintings have been compared to the works of such famous artists as Georgia O'Keeffe and Claude Monet.

During the summer of 2001 Olivia began experimenting with oil paints. She also expanded the subject matter of her work to include portraits and abstracts. Nearly all of her paintings feature bright colors, which have become a sort of trademark for her. "She loves color, and she's sick of me saying, 'Let's get subtle with some shades,'" said her art teacher, Mary Kay Krell. "We'll get halfway through something, and it's very muted, and she can't stand it any longer. That's her youth."

The first major showing of Olivia's work took place in 2001 at Art in the Square, an annual art festival in Southlake that raises money for charity. The event attracts many fine artists from surrounding states, along with thousands of visitors. Olivia sold dozens of paintings at the festival for between $25 and $350 each. A few months later the 11-year-old was a featured artist at the Thurburn Gallery in Fort Worth, where her work sold for up to $1,000 per painting.

Raising Money to Aid the Children of Afghanistan

The terrorist attacks of September 11, 2001, affected Olivia as they did many other American children. She was stunned by the tragic events and longed to find some way to help the families of those killed in the attack. At the same time, she felt a surge of patriotism and wanted to express it. She soon found an outlet for her feelings. On October 11, 2001, President George W. Bush made a radio address in which he asked the children of the United States to donate money

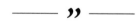

"My mom and I were driving to Wal-Mart, and President Bush was on the radio asking everyone to donate a dollar to America's fund for Afghan Children. I was very excited. I said, 'Oh my gosh. I want to do my part,'"Bennett remembered. "When I thought about how much freedom we have in this country, I really wanted to do something to help those children. I wanted to paint something big and powerful that would be my tribute to the victims and the heroes from September 11."

to help the children of Afghanistan, which the U.S. invaded because of its terrorist ties. "My mom and I were driving to Wal-Mart, and President Bush was on the radio asking everyone to donate a dollar to America's Fund for Afghan Children. I was very excited. I said, 'Oh my gosh. I want to do my part,'" Olivia remembered. "When I thought about how much freedom we have in this country, I really wanted to do something to help those children. I wanted to paint something big and powerful that would be my tribute to the victims and the heroes from September 11."

Olivia created a special painting called "Let Freedom Bloom," which shows a rose interwoven with the American flag. She made 199 limited-edition, signed prints and put them up for sale at $495 each. Within about six months, her efforts raised $33,000 for America's Fund for Afghan Children. Her goal was to raise $100,000 by the end of 2002. Thousands of other American children were also inspired to respond to President Bush's message. The fund ended up raising more than $4 million to buy winter clothing and medical supplies for the children of Afghanistan.

In recognition of her charitable contributions, Olivia was invited to meet President Bush in March 2002. She attended a speech at an elementary school in Virginia, during which the president publicly thanked her. "I wanted to single her out as someone who has done a little extra—not a little extra, a lot extra—for the fund to help Afghan boys and girls," Bush stated. Olivia had a chance to speak with the president afterward. "President Bush told me several times how beautiful he thinks the painting is, and that made me feel really good. He told me he thought it was a great way to help the charity and encouraged me to keep it going," she recalled. "It still hasn't sunk in that I actually met the president. It is just so cool. I have always said I wanted to meet the president, but I never thought I would be able to this soon."

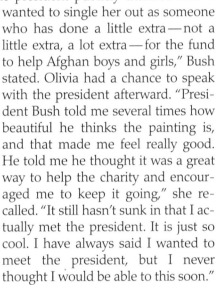

"President Bush told me several times how beautiful he thinks the painting is, and that made me feel really good," Bennett recalled. "It still hasn't sunk in that I actually met the president. It is just so cool."

In September 2002, Olivia was invited to New York City for ceremonies honoring the anniversary of September 11. She donated 3,000 prints of "Let Freedom Bloom" to the families of the victims of the terrorist attacks. It seems likely that her original painting will hang in the September 11 memorial when it is built.

A Promising Future

In 2002 Olivia began working with an agent, Ben Valenty of International Art and Entertainment, who represents other child art prodigies (young people with exceptional talents). "I've probably seen the portfolios of at least 5,000 kids, and many of them were extremely talented," Valenty stated. "But I have only seen what I consider to be a gift three times, and in Olivia's case, I think it is the most profound gift I've ever seen."

A Life In Full Bloom

The Story and Paintings of

Olivia Bennett

In July 2002 Olivia was invited to appear on a special edition of the "Oprah Winfrey Show" dedicated to child prodigies. She ended up selling several paintings to members of Winfrey's staff, and one of her works now hangs in the show's offices. In the fall of 2002 Olivia published a book called *A Life in Full Bloom: The Story and Paintings of Olivia Bennett*. The book tells about her battle with leukemia and her development as an artist, and it also features color reproductions of 40 of her works. "To say I'm going to have a book coming out is a great accomplishment," she noted. "To go to a store and see it on the shelf is going to be a great feeling."

Olivia says that an average painting takes between five and seven hours to complete, although some take over 20 hours. She usually paints late at night in an art studio above the garage in her family's home. Sometimes her mother reads aloud to her while she works. Although prints of her

paintings now sell for $500, and original canvases sell for $10,000 to $15,000, Olivia claims that the money is not important to her. "I love to paint," she stated. "I see things — a flower or a frog or a violin — and it's like they're saying, 'Paint me. Paint me.' Because they're just so beautiful, and I feel as though I'm just driven to paint them. It's like a bolt of lightning. I just have to do it. . . . I think no matter what, I would have become an artist. Being sick just kind of helped me discover my passion sooner rather than later. And it helped me really focus in a way that just a typical life without cancer might not have. And it made me really appreciate that every moment is a unique and rare opportunity, and I should just take advantage of that."

HOME AND FAMILY

Olivia Bennett continues to live in Southlake with her family. Her parents — neither of whom are artists — are continually amazed by her talent. "Just the other day I was watching her paint, and I was thinking to myself, 'Who is this person?'" her mother noted. "Just within a few paintings she had evolved so much it just blew me away." As Olivia's art gets more and more attention, her parents try to keep her grounded. They never push her to paint and instead encourage her to go to the mall and live the life of a normal teenager.

WRITINGS

A Life in Full Bloom: The Story and Paintings of Olivia Bennett, 2002 (with Derek Partridge)

FURTHER READING

Books

Bennett, Olivia, and Derek Partridge. *A Life in Full Bloom: The Story and Paintings of Olivia Bennett,* 2002

Periodicals

Dallas Morning News, Feb. 21, 2002, p.A21; Mar. 22, 2002, p.N1; Apr. 21, 2002, p.S1
Fort Worth Star-Telegram, Feb. 12, 2002, Metro sec., p.3; July 22, 2002, Metro sec., p.10
Houston Chronicle, Mar. 23, 2002, p.1
Teen People, Apr. 2003, p.145

Online Articles

http://www.mothernaturesparadise.com/
(*Mother Nature's Menagerie,* "Olivia Bennett," 2002)
http://www.boeing.com/
(*Boeing Global Advertising,* "Olivia Bennett: Painter" and "Olivia Bennett Radio Essay Transcript," 2003)

Further information for this profile was gathered from interviews with Bennett that aired on the *Today Show,* Mar. 21, 2002, and on the *Oprah Winfrey Show,* July 11, 2002.

ADDRESS

Olivia Bennett
International Art and Entertainment
23121 Antonio Parkway
Suite 140
Rancho Santa Margarita, CA 92688

WORLD WIDE WEB SITE

http://oliviabennett.com/

Vincent Brooks 1959?-

U.S. Army Brigadier General
Deputy Director of Operations for U.S. Central
Command during the 2003 War in Iraq

BIRTH

Vincent Brooks was born in about 1959 in Anchorage, Alaska. His parents are Leo A. Brooks, who was a major general in the U.S. Army, and Naomi (Lewis) Brooks, a teacher. Vincent has two siblings. His brother, Leo, Jr., is a year older and, like his brother, is a brigadier general in the Army. He currently serves as commandant of cadets at the U.S. Military Academy at West Point. Vincent's younger sister, Marquita, is a lawyer.

After retiring from the military, Vincent's father, Leo Brooks, became managing director for the city of Philadelphia. In May 1985 he found himself in the national media spotlight due to a violent confrontation between city authorities and a radical anti-government group called MOVE. At that time, MOVE members lived in a row house in Philadelphia. On May 13, 1985, MOVE members opened fire on police from their rooftop. After a long gun battle, the police dropped a bomb on the building. The bomb missed its target and sparked a fire that soon raged out of control. The blaze eventually burned an entire city block, leaving 250 people homeless and killing 11 people. Brooks and other city authorities were blamed by some people for the disaster. He left the job soon afterward, but was later cleared of any legal responsibility for the bombing.

YOUTH AND EDUCATION

The Brooks family is very private, so little information about Vincent's early years has been made public. It is known, however, that during his childhood, his father received military assignments that took him all across the country. With each new assignment, his family left friends and familiar surroundings behind in order to accompany him. As a result, all of the Brooks children attended several different schools during their childhood years. But Leo and Naomi Brooks did not permit their children to use the relocations as an excuse for poor school work. Instead, they set very high standards for their children. If one of them brought home a report card with all As and a B, their father would encourage the child to pull that B up to an A.

——— " ———

"We were all very, very close," recalled Marquita Brooks. "My parents always did things with us."

——— " ———

The family eventually settled in Sacramento, California, where both Brooks and his brother attended Jesuit High School. The school had very high academic standards and emphasized values that were similar to those the brothers had been taught at home, particularly hard work and self-discipline. "That high school," Leo Brooks later said, "was fundamentally a big part of helping prepare us to do what we were able to do." Besides Brooks and his older brother, only two other black students were enrolled at the school. But Vincent Brooks thrived at the school, posting outstanding grades and emerging as a leader of the school's basketball and track teams. He graduated from St. Jesuit in 1976.

During his high school years, Brooks had pondered a future career as a doctor. He received a basketball scholarship offer from North Carolina State University. But during Christmas break of his senior year, his older brother arrived home for the holidays from the U.S. Military Academy in New York. This military college, usually called West Point after the city where it is located, trains students to be officers in the U.S. Army. Brooks was tremendously impressed by the changes he saw in his older brother after only a few months at West Point. Leo was in top physical condition and looked "sharp" in his uniform, as Brooks later recalled. He also noted that Leo and his roommate, who had been invited to join the Brooks family for Christmas, carried themselves with confidence and pride. Later that evening, Brooks tried on his brother's West Point uniform for himself. "That night, when we went to bed," his father recalls, "I said I thought he was hooked [on going to West Point]."

> **"**
>
> *Vincent Brooks was tremendously impressed by the changes he saw in his older brother Leo after only a few months at West Point. When Leo came home at Christmas, Vincent tried on his brother's West Point uniform for himself. "That night, when we went to bed," his father recalls, "I said I thought he was hooked [on going to West Point]."*
>
> **"**

Over the next few days, Brooks admitted to his brother that the idea of attending West Point had become more attractive to him than the idea of studying medicine. The application deadline for enrolling at West Point had already passed, but Leo spoke to the basketball coach at the military academy and showed him a video of his younger brother playing basketball for Jesuit High. Brooks's basketball abilities and his fine academic record convinced academy administrators to admit him without delay.

Brooks made an immediate impact at West Point. He made the varsity basketball team as a freshman and excelled in his studies. In addition, he became known among the other cadets for his easygoing manner and good sense of humor During his senior year, he was selected as First Captain, a position similar to that of class president. The selection process to fill this position of honor was quite rigorous. Brooks and other candidates for the post underwent a series of interviews, and each candidate was evaluated on their leadership qualities and their military, academic, and physical performance. Brooks's selection

Brooks and General Tommy Franks (left) update news reporters on the progress of the war in Iraq in a March 2003 press conference.

made him the first African-American cadet to assume the prestigious post in the 177-year history of the academy.

As soon as the news of his appointment appeared in the papers, Brooks learned that being in the spotlight has its drawbacks. He received hate mail from racists—both inside and outside of the academy—who were angered at West Point's decision to appoint a black cadet to such an important position. Brooks initially was shocked by the negative reaction. After all, he had grown up in integrated military neighborhoods, where families of different ethnic backgrounds lived, worked, and played together. He also was amazed that some people would dismiss his many accomplishments simply because of the color of his skin. But Brooks did not wilt under these hateful statements. Instead, the publicity surrounding the issue taught him how to handle media attention and pressure in a calm and graceful manner.

In 1980 Brooks graduated from West Point first in his class with a Bachelor of Science (B.S.) degree. He went on to earn a Master's Degree in Military Art and Science from the School of Advanced Military Studies at the U.S. Army's Command and General Staff College in Fort Leavenworth, Kansas. He later was awarded a National Security Fellowship to study at Harvard University's John F. Kennedy School of Government. While serving in the military, he returned to school to attend the U.S. Army War College in Pennsylvania, graduating in 1999.

Brooks holds up a 55-card deck of cards featuring members of Iraq's leadership to reporters covering the war. The top card on the deck is of Iraqi President Saddam Hussein — the Ace of Spades.

CAREER HIGHLIGHTS

A Career in the Infantry

Brooks began his military career as a second lieutenant in the infantry (the division of the Army to which foot soldiers belong), but rose quickly through the ranks. Unlike his brother Leo, who had trained in light infantry, Brooks pursued a career in heavy artillery, the maintenance and operation of large-caliber guns.

Brooks's duties took him to a number of places in the world where the U.S. Army maintains a strong military presence, including Panama, Europe, South Korea, and the Middle East. In many of these assignments during the 1980s and 1990s, his responsibilities included commanding troops as well as helping shape U.S. military policy. Although no detailed information is available about these postings, it is known that Brooks served with the 82nd Airborne Division, the 1st Infantry Division, and the 3rd Army in Kuwait, where the first Gulf War took place in 1991. He reached the rank of major with the 1st Cavalry Division in the early 1990s. As the decade unfolded, he received new assignments at military bases across North, South, and Central America. At every stop, he impressed his superiors with his intelligence and dedication to duty. "He is a no-nonsense leader who has studied his profession carefully, works hard, and delivers," recalled retired general Wesley Clark.

Brooks interrupted his military service to attend the U.S. Army War College in Pennsylvania. After graduating in 1999, he reported to Fort Stewart, Georgia, where he served as 1st Brigade commander in the 3rd Infantry Division. During his time at Fort Stewart, Brooks led 3,000 soldiers on a peacekeeping mission in the former Yugoslav province of Kosovo, which had been torn apart by ethnic conflicts in the late 1990s. His work brought him in contact with General Tommy Franks, who later became the top military commander of U.S. forces during the 2003 invasion of Iraq.

Brooks points to a map of Iraq during an April 2003 news conference on the U.S.-led invasion of Iraq.

After completing his assignment in Kosovo, Brooks was promoted to a job at the Pentagon in Washington, D.C., the headquarters of the U.S. Department of Defense. He held a number of positions there, including deputy director for political-military affairs at the Joint Chiefs of Staff. In June 2002 Brooks was nominated for a promotion to the rank of brigadier general. At 43, he was the youngest of that year's 38 nominees to achieve this honor. His nomination was later confirmed by the U.S. Senate. With his promotion, the Brooks family became the first African-American family in U.S. military history with three generals from two different generations.

Briefing the World on the War in Iraq

In January 2003 Brooks learned that he would be leaving the Pentagon. General Franks had selected him to work as deputy director of operations for the U.S. Central Command (known as CENTCOM) headquarters in Doha, Qatar. CENTCOM, which usually operates out of Tampa, Florida, is a group that represents all of the U.S. armed services. It is responsible for overseeing military, political, and economic events in various parts of the world.

This assignment came at a time when the United States was preparing for war in Iraq. According to U.S. political and military leaders, Iraq and its president, Saddam Hussein, posed a great threat to the United States and other nations. They claimed that Iraq supported terrorism, and that it possessed weapons of mass destruction.

Brooks knew that as deputy director of operations, he would be responsible for explaining the progress of the war to journalists. At times, this can be a tremendously challenging task. After all, military spokesmen are responsible for informing the public about the military's actions. But they also need to keep silent about some aspects of military operations to ensure the safety of soldiers. In addition, spokesmen must keep in mind that public support for wars and other military actions often depends on the tone and content of the news they read and watch on television. Reporters, on the other hand, have a professional duty to investigate stories and confirm the claims that government spokesmen make. In fact, they play a vital role in ensuring that the American public receives accurate information about issues and events around the world. At times, the differing goals of spokespersons and reporters can create tensions and conflict between the two parties.

> "My son is not a hero," said Brooks's father. "Those kids getting shot at and killed are. I will not exploit the hunger for knowledge, nor slip into a gloat for my son or my family, while other families weep."

In March 2003, U.S. troops invaded Iraq. As the war unfolded, Brooks emerged as one of the military's most visible spokespersons. General Franks was uncomfortable in front of television cameras and did not enjoy answering reporters' questions. Brooks, on the other hand, seemed born to the task. His imposing physical appearance and ability to express himself clearly made him the perfect spokesperson for the military. For example, he explained the significance of battlefield slides and videos that were shown at the U.S. military's daily press briefings with great ease. Everyone who watched the daily briefings on television, which were broadcast live every weekday morning and then repeated throughout the day, was impressed by his intelligence and composure.

What's more, Brooks actually seemed to enjoy fielding questions from reporters, even when they were critical of military actions and decisions. Observers noted that he handled these comments with patience and good humor. For example, during a briefing early in the war one of the reporters complained that General Franks himself should be telling them what was going on. Brooks responded, "He's fighting a war now. And he has me to

Brooks fielded questions from dozens of reporters during his sessions with the media.

do this for him." Some of the journalists who attended Brooks's daily briefings were frustrated because his answers to specific questions about casualties and troop movements were often vague. One reporter described his manner as "robotic" because he tended to use standard phrases that sounded as though they had been "scripted" by his superiors. But he also showed a flair for expressing himself in a way that was almost poetic. At one point, for example, he compared America's military might to a "dagger" that was "clearly pointed at the heart of the Baghdad regime."

Brooks quickly became one of the war's most visible African-American faces, along with Secretary of State Colin Powell and National Security Advisor Condoleeza Rice. Brooks also served as a reminder that the forces fighting in Iraq reflected the diversity of the American population. Soon after he began appearing on television, he and his family members were bombarded with requests for interviews, most of which they turned down. Brooks's father summed up the family's feelings when he said that "My son is not a hero. Those kids getting shot at and killed are. I will not exploit the hunger for knowledge, nor slip into a gloat for my son or my family, while other families weep. When the war is over, I will speak."

Brooks is aware that he has become a role model for young African-Americans who are thinking about a career in the military. But he has never thought of himself as a celebrity. Raised by his parents to believe that he could accomplish anything if he gave his best effort, he suggests that discipline and sacrifice are the keys to success for others as well. In this regard, Brooks agrees that his life can be an example to others, especially young people. "People can see the achievement and how hard work leads to it," he said.

On April 24, 2003, Brooks concluded his duties as CENTCOM's spokesman. He returned to the United States, where he was assigned to the Pentagon.

Brooks agrees that his life can be an example for young people. "People can see the achievement and how hard work leads to it," he said.

MARRIAGE AND FAMILY

When he is not serving overseas with the military, Brooks lives in northern Virginia with his wife, Carol, who is a physical therapist, and their four daughters.

HOBBIES AND OTHER INTERESTS

Brooks routinely works long days, so he says that his favorite way of relaxing is to "hang out with my wife." He describes himself as a "hopeless romantic" who loves nothing better than spending an evening on the sofa with his wife watching "Def Comedy Jam" or a movie. "Anything she's interested in," he says, "is good enough for me."

FURTHER READING

Periodicals

Chicago Sun-Times, Mar. 27, 2003, p.8
Current Biography Yearbook, 2003
Financial Times (London), Apr. 26, 2003, p.25
Jet, Apr. 21, 2003, p.8
New York Times, Apr. 4, 2003, p.B11
Philadelphia Inquirer, Apr. 10, 2003, p.D1
Sacramento Bee, Apr. 1, 2003, p.A10
Washington Post, May 22, 2003, p.T14

Online Articles

http://www.africana.com
  (*Africana.com,* "Who is Brigadier General Vincent Brooks?"
  Apr. 9, 2003)
http://www.cnn.com
  (*CNN.com,* "Military Man Brooks Steps Up to the Mike,"
  April 8, 2003)
http://www.sacobserver.com
  (*Sacramento Observer Online,* "General Brooks: Why Be Discredited for
  Excelling?" Apr. 28, 2003)
http://www.usma.edu
  (*USMA In The News,* "One Black Family, Three Generals: Brooks
  Brothers Reared in Military Tradition," Apr. 1, 2003)
http://dynamic.washtimes.com
  (*The Washington Times,* "Honorably Speaking," Apr. 11, 2003)

ADDRESS

Vincent Brooks
Room 2-E949
The Pentagon
Arlington, VA 20301

Amanda Bynes 1986-

American Actress
Star of the TV Shows "All That," "The Amanda Show,"
and "What I Like about You," as Well as the Movies
Big Fat Liar and *What a Girl Wants*

BIRTH

Amanda Laura Bynes was born on April 3, 1986, in Thousand
Oaks, California. She lives with her father, Rick Bynes, who is
a dentist, and her mother, Lynn Bynes, who helps manage the
dental office. Bynes is the youngest of three children. She has
an older sister, Jillian, and an older brother, Tom.

YOUTH

Bynes displayed a natural talent and enthusiam for entertaining people from a very early age. Funny and uninhibited, she proved to be a natural crowd-pleaser at the dinner table and other family gatherings. "I guess I've always liked to make people laugh, ever since I was real little," Bynes said. Her father, meanwhile, often told friends that he wished that famous film director Steven Spielberg would drop by so that he could show off his precocious youngest daughter.

By age seven, Bynes had developed a deep interest in the theatre. She even learned to recite lines from plays in which her older sister was performing. At age seven she performed on stage herself for the first time, playing the role of the young orphan Molly in a local theatre production of *Annie*. As time passed, Bynes took part in other productions as well. For example, in 1995 she played Scout in a stage production of *To Kill a Mockingbird*. That same year, she took the role of Mary in the play *The Secret Garden*. Bynes admitted that her involvement in these productions required her to spend a lot of hours rehearsing and performing. But she claimed that she loved every moment. "Some kids like doing sports, and some kids like singing," she explained. "I just always liked to perform."

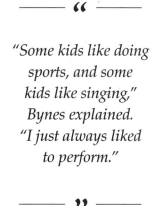

"Some kids like doing sports, and some kids like singing," Bynes explained. "I just always liked to perform."

In 1996 Bynes's parents enrolled her in a children's "comedy camp" that was being held at a Los Angeles comedy club. At the end of the camp, all of the children performed for their teachers and parents. When Bynes's turn came to march out on the stage, she performed a skit about school that she had written with help from her dad. Unbeknownest to her, two television producers from the Nickelodeon television network were in the audience, scouting for new talent. Both of the producers, Dan Schneider and Brian Robbins, were bowled over by Bynes's performance. According to Robbins, Bynes was "a tiny little thing with a wonderful sense of irony and comic timing." Schneider was impressed as well. "When I saw her on stage, she was the size of an avocado," he said. "But she was hysterical, and just totally won over the audience. And we had her come in and audition."

If Bynes was nervous about auditioning for a spot on Nickelodeon, she did not show it. Instead, she skillfully delivered over four pages of dialogue in front of a camera and a live audience. Schneider and Robbins were delighted with the performance, which confirmed their belief that they had discovered a naturally funny, talented, and likable girl. They immediately offered her a role in the Nick sketch comedy show "All That," where she spent the next three years honing her skills as an actress and comedian.

EDUCATION

Bynes never let her love for performing interfere with her studies. On the contrary, she posted straight As not only in English—her favorite subject—but also in other classes. As Bynes's career in entertainment blossomed, however, she and her parents realized that it would be difficult for her to maintain a regular school schedule. With this in mind, they arranged for a private tutor for the young actress. Throughout Bynes's years at Nickelodeon, she began each morning with a long session with her tutor. She continued to use a private tutor after leaving Nick to pursue other television and film opportunities.

CAREER HIGHLIGHTS

One of Nickelodeon's Brightest Stars

Bynes joined the cast of the Nickelodeon television show "All That" in 1995. She spent the next several years working with other child actors on the variety show, which featured a group of young performers doing short comedy scenes. The series was aimed at young adolescents—"tweens" making the transition between childhood and the teen years. By the end of her first year on the show, Bynes had emerged as one of the show's most popular performers. Indeed, some of the roles she played—such as a starship commander named Captain Tantrum and Ashley the obnoxious advice columnist—ranked among the most popular characters on the show. In 1997 she even earned a Cable Ace Award nomination in recognition of her comic contributions to the show.

Bynes admitted that the demands of performing on a television series sometimes exhausted her. "Memorizing lines can be difficult," she noted. "It's hard when I have to go home and say to myself, 'Okay, Amanda, you've got to get the lines in your head!' Sometimes I try to write my lines down from memory. It's kind of like studying for a test."

Fortunately, Bynes's enthusiasm for her work always kept her in a positive frame of mind. In fact, she exhibited a strong determination to improve her skills as an actor. For example, during her years on "All That" she worked very hard to strengthen her comic timing and her delivery of lines. She did

Bynes relaxes with a book at her home in California.

not want to always rely on acting coaches or the director for guidance on her performance. Schneider and Robbins, meanwhile, expressed amazement at their young star's ability to handle anything they threw at her. "I've never written a part for her she couldn't pull off," declared Schneider.

In 1997 Bynes moved on to a new Nickelodeon game show called "Figure It Out," although she continued to make appearances on "All That" through 2000. On "Figure It Out," a panel of kids affiliated with the Nickelodeon network faced off against kid contestants with a secret talent or accomplishment. On each episode, the panelists quizzed the guest with questions in an effort to guess their secret — and avoid getting "slimed" with gallons of colorful goo. Bynes appeared regularly on "Figure It Out" from 1997 to 2000, showcasing a funny and exuberant personality that further boosted her popularity with Nickelodeon viewers.

"The Amanda Show"

In 1999 Nickelodeon decided to make Bynes the host and main attraction of a new comedy-variety television show patterned as a kids' version of "Saturday Night Live." This show, called "The Amanda Show" in honor of Bynes, featured comedy sketches and musical acts aimed at young audi-

Bynes poses for the camera on the set of "The Amanda Show,"
which broadcast on Nickelodeon from 1999 to 2002.

ences. "The first time I got the script, it said, 'The Amanda Show' on it," Bynes remembered. "I thought they were kidding. I'm still little Amanda, and to be getting my own show, it's like, oh, my gosh!"

When "The Amanda Show" premiered on Nickelodeon in October 1999, the 13-year-old Bynes became the youngest host of a weekly network show in television history. The program and its likable star immediately attracted big audiences. Each show began with Bynes delivering a stand-up monologue, then progressed with a series of comic skits and musical numbers. As the show progressed, Bynes developed a number of popular recurring characters, including Moody Fallon, part of a gang of teens based on the characters from the television series "Dawson's Creek." Other silly characters played by Bynes included the celebrity-obsessed Penolope Taynt and stern Judge Trudy.

Even as "The Amanda Show" brought Bynes legions of new Nick fans, however, she explored other career opportunities as well. In late 1999, for example, she appeared on the HBO program "Arli$$" as a star ice skater who discovers that her parents are stealing her earnings. This guest role marked Bynes's first appearance on a program for adults.

Balancing Fame and Normal Life

By 2000, Bynes had emerged as one of the country's most successful and popular young entertainers. That year she was honored at the Nickelodeon Kids Choice Awards as Favorite TV Actress (the first of four consecutive awards in this category). Soon, offers to appear on other television shows began to pile up. But she didn't let her rising popularity affect her. She claimed that she still preferred "jeans and a t-shirt" to any other type of clothing, and she made a special effort to maintain her friendships with people outside of the entertainment world. "When I'm at work, I'm 'Work

"When I'm at work, I'm 'Work Amanda,' but when I come home and talk to all my friends, I'm 'Regular Amanda,'"Bynes said. "My friends come to tapings of my show and hang out afterward. We never talk about show business. We talk about a lot more important things, like shopping and boys."

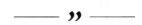

Amanda,' but when I come home and talk to all my friends, I'm 'Regular Amanda,'" she explained. "My friends come to tapings of my show and hang out afterward. We never talk about show business. We talk about a lot more important things, like shopping and boys."

Bynes's family also has helped her stay grounded by treating her just like a normal teen-ager. "I think my parents are a big part of that because I'm still a normal kid," she said. "I can't do whatever I want! . . . Just like anyone else, [my parents] make important decisions for me. I'm a normal teen, and I have to listen to what they say." Bynes admitted, however, that she sometimes feels the normal teen resentment of parental authority. "Like there are times I get frustrated because I want to wear certain shoes and they don't want me to wear them. It's all good in the end because I realize that there will be a time and place for high shoes. . . . I wouldn't say I

was a different person at home, but I don't have a job at home and my parents make me do the exact same things like before I was on TV. I wake up and I'm the exact same lazy person who doesn't want to make her bed. That would be me!"

For their part, members of Bynes's family, who refer to her by the affectionate nickname "Chicky," have repeatedly expressed pride in the way their youngest member has handled the celebrity limelight. "The great thing about Amanda is that she doesn't have a Hollywood attitude," said her brother Tom. "She does her thing on camera, and when she's done she comes home and she's just an ordinary kid."

Breaking Into the Movies

In 2001, Bynes was approached to star in a feature film called *Big Fat Liar,* co-starring Frankie Muniz, the well-known star of the "Malcom in the Middle" television series. Bynes jumped at the opportunity, eager to accept the challenge of a role in a major motion picture. "People don't recognize I'm getting older," she said. "They see reruns of 'All That' so they assume I'm ten years old. I'm 16. I'm almost 5 [feet], 8 [inches]. I'm driving now."

"Frankie [Muniz] and I had a lot of fun doing the movie," Bynes recalled. "We had golf carts in the movie, so sometimes we would steal them and drive around the Universal backlot. It was very fun."

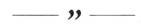

Released in 2002, *Big Fat Liar* concerns a boy (played by Muniz) who constantly gets himself into trouble with his lies. When he writes a story about this terrible habit, a producer steals his idea to make a hit movie. Outraged, the boy tells everyone about the producer's actions, only to find that no one believes him. This leads him and his best friend, played by Bynes, to take off for Hollywood to get revenge. The rest of the movie is about their adventures as they track the producer down. "Frankie and I had a lot of fun doing the movie," recalled Bynes. "We had golf carts in the movie, so sometimes we would steal them and drive around the Universal backlot. It was very fun—we had fun doing that, I must say."

Big Fat Liar proved to be a nice moneymaker for Universal Studios. It cost only $15 million to make, but earned over $50 million. The movie gathered only mixed reviews, but most critics agreed that Bynes's performance as the spunky, spirited sidekick was one of the film's highlights.

The year 2002 also marked Bynes's departure from Nickelodeon. She recognized that she owed her thriving career to shows such as "All That" and "The Amanda Show," but she knew that she needed to select more

The WB series "What I Like About You" features Wesley Jonathan (left),
Bynes (front left), Jennie Garth (front right), and Simon Rex (right).

grown-up roles. With this in mind, Bynes accepted a starring role in a new situation comedy (sitcom) called "What I Like About You" on the Warner Brothers (WB) television network.

In the show, which also features former "Beverly Hills 90210" star Jennie Garth, Bynes plays 16-year-old Holly, a spirited girl who has to move in with her uptight older sister (played by Garth) in Manhattan when her dad leaves for a job in Japan. Many of the show's early episodes highlighted Bynes's talent for slapstick comedy, while simultaneously exploring the deepening relationship between the two siblings. The show immediately proved popular with young viewers, and critics praised Bynes for her energetic performances. The *Los Angeles Times,* for example, declared that "Bynes handles the quick-tempo comic bantering [in the show] like the seasoned pro she already is."

What a Girl Wants

Bynes's hot streak continued in 2003 with her starring role in *What a Girl Wants,* a major motion picture that also featured Colin Firth and Kelly Preston. A remake of an older movie and play called *The Reluctant Debutante,* it featured Bynes as a girl named Daphne who has grown up in New York City with her free-spirited mother. She has never known her father, a haughty English lord played by Firth. In fact, Firth's character is not even aware that his brief marriage to Daphne's mother 17 years earlier produced a daughter. As the film unfolds, Daphne decides that she can't move on with life until she meets her father, so she flies off to London to introduce herself. The result is an amusing clash between Daphne's outgoing American ways and the stiff British manners of her father and his extended family.

> ———— **"** ————
>
> *"We captured [Bynes] just at the moment she's becoming a woman, and of course, she has this amazingly huge following, so once we knew she was interested, it was a slam-dunk," said Dennie Gordon, director of* **What a Girl Wants.** *"This is the movie where she gets to show that she's a big, grown-up young lady who can both wear ball gowns [yet] look fabulous in T-shirt and jeans."*
>
> ———— **"** ————

Director Dennie Gordon was thrilled that Bynes agreed to play the part of Daphne. "When I met Amanda, she was so clearly this girl," Gordon recalled. "She's worldly, yet still in awe of the world. We captured her just at the moment she's becoming a woman, and of course she has this amazingly huge following, so once we knew she was interested, it was a slam-dunk. This is the movie where she gets to show that she's a big, grown-up young lady who can both wear ball gowns (yet) look fabulous in T-shirt and jeans."

Bynes dances the night away in a scene from What a Girl Wants *(2003).*

Bynes and co-star Colin Firth in What a Girl Wants.

What a Girl Wants received a generally warm reception from critics, who saw it as an upbeat comedy especially well-suited to girls in their early to mid-teens. Most reviewers singled out Bynes's bubbly performance as the key to the movie's appeal. *Entertainment Weekly* observed that "in her sassy but scrubbed way, Bynes is a real charmer." The *Cincinnati Enquirer*, meanwhile, described her as "an appealing and energetic leading lady."

According to Bynes, her starring role in *What a Girl Wants* was a perfect match for her long-term career plans. "I want to be looked at as an adult actress," she said. "That's why I didn't want to do a big movie when I was 11. I was waiting till I was a little bit older." With this goal in mind, Bynes made numerous appearances on more adult-oriented programs in 2002 and 2003. In 2003 alone, for example, she appeared on "The Tonight Show with Jay Leno," cohosted MTV's "Total Request Live," and served as a presenter at the MTV Music Awards.

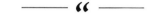

"You can watch the re-runs of 'I Love Lucy,' and it's just as good as the first time you saw it," Bynes said. *"[Lucille Ball is] kind of my idol—just go for the laughs, and don't worry about what you look like."*

MAJOR INFLUENCES

Bynes enjoys watching many actors and actresses, including Jim Carrey, Kirsten Dunst, Kevin Kline, Lisa Kudrow, Carol Burnett, Cameron Diaz, and Martin Short. But she claims that the actress who has inspired her the most in her own career is legendary comedian Lucille Ball. "You can watch the re-runs of 'I Love Lucy,' and it's just as good as the first time you saw it," Bynes declared. "She's kind of my idol—just go for the laughs, don't worry about what you look like."

HOBBIES AND OTHER INTERESTS

Bynes has many interests besides acting, including swimming, shopping, drawing, painting, writing, and reading. "I love the dictionary!" she has declared. "I love words and books. . . . I read right before bed mostly, and I feel like I have to know what every word means so I keep my dictionary next to me. I don't know why, I just have this fascination." She also likes word games like Scrabble and Jumble: "They're good for the mind," she says.

Another one of Bynes's passions is sketching fashion designs. "I've been drawing since kindergarten," she noted. "As I watch a fashion show or an

Bynes and actor Jim Carrey laugh it up during a May 15, 2003, appearance on the "Tonight Show."

award show, I copy what I see. The Oscars have the newest fashions — that's the show I look forward to the most." Bynes claims that she has filled 50 sketch books with designs over the years. "My mom's artistic and my dad's funny, so I guess that's where I get it from," she said.

Bynes's favorite foods include pizza, hamburgers, mint chocolate and malt ball crunch ice cream, stir-fry vegetables, pasta, and chicken Caesar salad. She also enjoys all types of music, from current bands like the Dave Matthews Band, No Doubt, Blink 182, Britney Spears, Pink, and 'N Sync to older performers such as James Taylor and Sting.

SELECTED CREDITS

Movies

Big Fat Liar, 2002
What a Girl Wants, 2003
Charlotte's Web 2, 2003 (voice of Nellie)

Television

"All That," 1996-2000
"Figure It Out," 1997-2000

"The Amanda Show," 1999-2002
"What I Like About You," 2002-
"Rugrats," 2002- (as voice of Taffy)

HONORS AND AWARDS

Nickelodeon Kid's Choice Award: 2000, 2001, 2002, and 2003, Favorite TV
   Actress
Nickelodeon Kid's Choice Award: 2003, Favorite Movie Actress

FURTHER READING

Periodicals

American Girl, Jan./Feb. 2000, p.12
Cincinnati Enquirer, Apr. 4, 2003, p.A5
Detroit News, Nov. 28, 2002, p.G5
Entertainment Weekly, Apr. 11, 2003, p.57
Los Angeles Times, Apr. 4, 2003, p.15; May 2, 2003, p.E30
McCalls, Dec. 2000, p.42
New York Daily News, Feb. 4, 2002, p.35
New York Times, Oct. 20, 2002, p.B27
Teen Magazine, Apr. 2002, p.48
Time, Apr. 14, 2003, p. 76
Washington Post, Nov. 17, 2000, p.C11

ADDRESS

Amanda Bynes
Warner Brothers
4000 Warner Blvd.
Burbank, CA 91522

WORLD WIDE WEB SITES

http://thewb.com
http://whatagirlwantsmovie.warnerbros.com
http://www.nick.com

Josh Hartnett 1978-

American Actor
Star of the Hit Films *Pearl Harbor, O,* and
Black Hawk Down

BIRTH

Joshua Daniel Hartnett was born on July 21, 1978, in St. Paul,
Minnesota. His father, Daniel Hartnett, is a former professional guitar player who later became a building manager.
His mother is a teaching assistant. Josh's parents divorced
when he was quite young, and his mother moved to San Francisco, California. Josh was raised primarily by his father and

stepmother, Molly, who is an artist. He has three younger siblings: Jessica, Jake, and Joe.

YOUTH

The Hartnett family has lived in St. Paul since 1865. Josh's great-great-grandfather went to Minnesota to work on the railroads, and his mother's family arrived in St. Paul around 1900. He grew up, therefore, with a deep attachment to the Minneapolis-St. Paul area.

Josh first learned what it was like to perform in front of an audience by serving as an altar boy. He and his friends often volunteered to serve as altar boys at funerals because they would be paid five dollars and get a day off school. When he was a little older, he worked in a video store, and this is where he fell in love with movies. He even remembered saying to himself, "People in Hollywood are doing work like that? I want to go out there!" Josh's father recognized his interest in the entertainment business and suggested classic movies that he should check out. To this day, Hartnett idolizes Jimmy Stewart, the actor who starred in many of the films he watched as a youngster.

When he was 16, Hartnett and some of his friends made a short film about a robbery at a Dairy Queen—until a passerby thought a real robbery was taking place and called the police. "It's a good thing we were taking a break and eating Dilly Bars [when the police arrived]," recalled Hartnett. "If we'd had our fake yellow pistols in our hands, we probably would have all been goners."

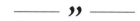

When he was 16, Hartnett acted in a short film that he and some of his friends made about a robbery at a Dairy Queen. His performance as one of the robbers was so convincing that a passerby thought a real robbery was taking place and called the police. "It's a good thing we were taking a break and eating Dilly Bars [when the police arrived]," he recalled. "If we'd had our fake yellow pistols in our hands, we probably would have all been goners."

EDUCATION

Hartnett attended Nativity of Our Lord School in St. Paul before starting high school at Cretin-Derham Hall. At the end of his sophomore year, he transferred to South High School in Minneapolis, which was known for putting on three or four huge theatrical productions every year. His high school theater coach, Louise Bormann, remembers casting him as gambler Sky Masterston in the musical *Guys and Dolls*. Even at this young age, Hartnett showed impressive poise and professionalism. "It was like, 'Whoa! Here's a kid I don't need to coach,'" Bormann said.

Although Hartnett was an intelligent boy, he was a mediocre student. "I hated school," he admitted. "I loved learning, but I hated doing all the busywork." He was more interested in playing football, but he had to quit the team when he tore a ligament in his knee at 16. At this point his aunt, who was very interested in theater, talked him into auditioning at the Youth Performance Company. This community theater group for young actors in Minneapolis was putting on *Tom Sawyer.* Hartnett agreed to audition and ended up winning the role of Huckleberry Finn. "It started with me just being competitive and wanting to see if I could beat out the other kids," he acknowledged. "[But] I kind of just took to it. I loved the immediate gratification of being onstage."

> *Hartnett claims that his acting career "started with me just being competitive and wanting to see if I could beat out the other kids [for parts]. I kind of just took to it. I loved the immediate gratification of being onstage."*

By the time he graduated from South High School in June 1996, Hartnett had appeared in several television commercials and hired a manager who specialized in handling talented young Minnesota actors. He soon began attending the theater program at the State University of New York at Purchase, but he left before completing his freshman year because of a disagreement with the university's administrators. "They didn't really kick me out; they just said I could leave if I wanted to," Hartnett explained. Never an enthusiastic student, he decided to take his manager's advice and move to Los Angeles.

CAREER HIGHLIGHTS

The "Hottie of Horror"

Hartnett arrived in Los Angeles in February 1997. He immediately signed with a Hollywood- based agent and started going out for three or four auditions a day. "I was kind of a romantic and deluded kid," he admitted. "I

Josh Hartnett sits behind the wheel in a scene from The Faculty.

thought that I was going to walk in and say, 'I'm here.' And they'd be like, "You're our guy.'" In fact, Hartnett landed his first role—in the television detective drama "Cracker"—within a couple of months of his arrival in Los Angeles. He played the troubled 17-year-old son of a police psychologist. "My first scene on national television, I was sitting on a toilet," he recalled. "My dad said I could only go up from there." The show was canceled after nine episodes, but it gave Hartnett the introduction to Hollywood that he needed.

The cancellation of "Cracker" freed Hartnett to accept his first big screen role, as Jamie Lee Curtis's son in *Halloween: H20,* a teen slasher movie in the "Halloween" series. Curtis plays Laurie Strode, sister of the Halloween murderer Michael Myers. He is believed to be dead—but of course is very much alive. To escape from her homicidal brother, Laurie fakes her own death in a car accident, moves to California under an assumed name, and starts a new life as headmistress of an elite California boarding school. Most of the school's faculty and students go off on a camping trip to Yosemite. But Laurie's son John, played by Hartnett, manages to stay behind, putting himself in serious jeopardy. Although the movie itself received poor reviews, a critic from *Interview* magazine praised Hartnett for his "thoughtful, brooding presence tempered by good humor." He was also nominated for an MTV Movie Award for Best Breakthrough Performance.

Not long after the 1998 release of *Halloween: H20,* Hartnett appeared in another horror movie, *The Faculty.* This time the villain is an alien that shows up at a high school in Ohio and begins to take over first the faculty and then the students. Hartnett played Zeke Tyler, a drug-dealing underachiever who is repeating his senior year. Zeke unexpectedly rises to the challenge and decides to do something about the "invasion of the bodysnatchers" taking place at his school. This film received even worse reviews than *Halloween: H20,* but Hartnett's performance led *Seventeen* magazine to call him the "unofficial hottie of horror."

Branching Out

Hartnett recognized the danger in being typecast as a teenage horror movie star, so he made a deliberate effort to find roles that would broaden his acting experience. In 2000 he worked on five different films. The first, *Here on Earth,* provided him with an opportunity to play a romantic leading role. Hartnett played Jasper, a farm boy who is dating his childhood sweetheart, Samantha (played by Leelee Sobieski), a waitress at a local diner. His main rival for Samantha's affection is Kelley (played by Chris Klein), an arrogant preppy and class valedictorian. Kelley challenges Jasper to a drag race that ends up destroying the diner, which is owned by Samantha's mother. Their punishment is to rebuild the place, and Kelley moves in with Jasper and his family until the work is done. The developing relationships among the three teens provide the crux of the story. Like most of the films in which Hartnett had appeared to this point, *Here on Earth* was panned by the critics.

Soon after *Here on Earth* was released, Hartnett appeared in *Blow Dry.* He played an ambitious young hairdresser from Yorkshire, England, who enters a national hairstyling competition. The competition triggers an intense rivalry between two beauty salons in the same small town. Hartnett had to master a British accent for the role. It also gave him a chance to play opposite Rachel Leigh Cook, who graduated from the same Minneapolis high school as Hartnett, only two years later. Although the role was a departure for him, Hartnett was able to tap into his own competitiveness to play it convincingly. Still, the movie itself failed to attract much notice.

Hartnett's third movie of 2000, *The Virgin Suicides,* was the first film in which he appeared that earned wide critical acclaim. Adapted from a novel by Jeffrey Eugenides and directed by Sophia Coppola, daughter of the legendary director Francis Ford Coppola, the film tells the story of the five

Hartnett and co-star Julia Stiles at the premiere of the movie O.

mysterious Lisbon sisters. The youngest daughter kills herself, and the film explores the effect of her death on the remaining four sisters and their overly strict parents. The boys in their suburban Michigan neighborhood are fascinated by the Lisbon sisters—particularly Lux, the eldest (played by Kirsten Dunst)—and spend most of their time fantasizing about what might happen if the girls ever escaped their parents' control. Hartnett plays Tripp Fontaine, a 1970s teenage heartthrob who develops an obsession for Lux. Sophia Coppola cast him in the role without even meeting him in person. "You just knew he had it," she recalls. Although Dunst attracted most of the critical attention for her portrayal of Lux, Hartnett also received praise for his skillful portrayal of the seductive and irresponsible Tripp. (For more information on Dunst, see *Biography Today Performing Artists,* Vol. 1.)

The fourth movie that Hartnett worked on in 2000 was *Town & Country,* a divorce comedy that was not released until the following year. Hartnett plays a relatively minor role as the son of the film's two stars, Warren Beatty and Diane Keaton. The film follows two middle-aged couples and explores their marital problems. But despite a talented cast that also included Goldie

47

Hawn, Andie MacDowell, Garry Shandling, and Nastassja Kinski, *Town & Country* was a colossal failure among critics and at the box office.

Hartnett's fifth movie of 2000 was *O*, a modern-day retelling of Shakespeare's *Othello* set in an elite boarding school. "O" is the nickname of Odin James (Mekhi Phifer), the school's only black student and its star basketball player. O is in love with the dean's daughter, Desi (Desdemona in Shakespeare's original), played by Julia Stiles. The dean is torn between wanting to end his daughter's interracial romance and wanting the school's basketball team to win the state finals. Martin Sheen plays the school's basketball coach, and Hartnett plays the role of Hugo Goulding, the coach's son. Just like the character Iago in *Othello,* Hugo is jealous of O's stardom and the close relationship that develops between his father and the star athlete. As a result, Hugo tries to destroy O by convincing him that Desi is in love with another boy on the team, who happens to be O's best friend.

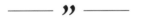

"I knew [Pearl Harbor] was going to be huge," Hartnett remembered. "I was afraid I wouldn't be able to walk around and live my life the way I always had."

Although *O* was filmed in 2000, its release was delayed until the summer of 2001. Many movie studio executives worried that the film's grim and violent ending was too similar to the real-life 1999 student shooting incident at Columbine High School in Colorado. The delay proved fortunate for Hartnett, because in the meantime he appeared in the blockbuster *Pearl Harbor* and became a star. But even though Hartnett's name brought his fans to the theaters, *O* was not well received by critics. *Variety* magazine attacked the film for its "thoroughly misguided effort to make a classic tale somehow topical and relevant."

Pearl Harbor

When Hartnett was first approached about appearing in *Pearl Harbor*—a big-budget action movie about the Japanese attack on the U.S. Navy base in Hawaii on December 7, 1941—he was hesitant about accepting the role. "I knew this movie was going to be huge," Hartnett explained. "I was afraid I wouldn't be able to walk around and live my life the way I always had." He went home to Minnesota and talked to his father about his fears. His father pointed out that fame was only temporary, but that the regret he might feel if he turned the role down could last a lifetime.

Producer Jerry Bruckheimer, cast members Josh Hartnett, Kate Beckinsale, and Ben Affleck, and director Michael Bay pose together prior to the world premiere of the motion picture Pearl Harbor.

Director Michael Bay had no hesitation at all about casting Hartnett in one of the lead roles. "He was this grunge kid from Minnesota," Bay recalls. "As soon as I screen-tested him, I knew. I got so excited. I called [producer Jerry Bruckheimer] on the phone. I said, 'Jerry, this guy is awesome.'" Still, Bay was determined not to hire the first young actor he saw. He kept Hartnett waiting for three months while he auditioned others. But the director ultimately gave Hartnett the role of Danny Walker, a young American fighter pilot who is stationed in Hawaii at the time of the Japanese attack. "He had comic timing, sincerity, and a genuine shyness that really worked," Bay says.

In the movie, Danny and Rafe (played by Ben Affleck) are ace fighter pilots and best friends. They also fall in love with the same woman, a young nurse named Evelyn (played by Kate Beckinsale). The resulting love triangle is played out against the backdrop of World War II and the attack on Pearl Harbor. To prepare for their roles as military men, Hartnett, Affleck, and several of the film's other actors were sent to an Army boot camp on the Hawaiian island of Oahu, where Pearl Harbor is located. "We were there for about four or five days and it felt like seven, eight, nine years,"

Hartnett said. "They were supposed to break us down and then build us up again like they do in the Army. They didn't have time to build us back up. They broke us down and said, 'Go, make a movie. Have fun.'" But Hartnett emerged from the experience with great respect for members of the military, whom he says "work harder than most people I've ever met."

Hartnett also learned a great deal from talking to World War II veterans about their experiences. "I talked for hours with a guy who was a number-one ace pilot in the Pacific, shooting down Japanese planes," he said. "We met right off the bat, but the conversation stuck with me throughout the whole film shoot."

Although *Pearl Harbor* received a huge amount of publicity and attracted many moviegoers, it received mixed reviews and never made the anticipated box-office history. It did, however, turn Josh Hartnett into a recognizable Hollywood name. When asked how he felt about the fact that the movie received some harsh reviews, Hartnett responded with characteristic nonchalance: "I don't want people to think that I'm ungrateful for what I've been given," he said. "But at the same time my life is not completely run by the movie business. I have friends and family that I really care about and lots of things that I love to do aside from this. So it's nice when things go well, and it's too bad when things don't."

40 Days and 40 Nights

After wrapping up *Pearl Harbor,* Hartnett switched gears and appeared in a lighthearted romantic comedy, *40 Days and 40 Nights.* His character, Matt Sullivan, has just gone through a bad breakup with his longtime girlfriend. He decides to give up sex for Lent, a 40-day period in which many Christians fast and ask forgiveness for their sins in preparation for Easter. Unfortunately, the day after he makes his decision he meets Erica (Shannyn Sossamon), the girl of his dreams. She and everyone around him — including his ex-girlfriend and his buddies at the office — seem determined to make him break his vow.

Hartnett tried to get into his role by abstaining from all sexual activity, even hugging and kissing, during the filming. But the main result of this decision was that he endured constant teasing from the cast and crew. "It was pretty much embarrassing for me from beginning to end," he recalled. However, he did appreciate the fact that the film gave him his first chance to play a comic leading role.

40 Days and 40 Nights aroused a certain amount of controversy upon its release, which took place during the middle of Lent. Some religious organizations objected to the film's subject matter and claimed that it was disrespectful of the traditions of Lent. It received only lukewarm reviews, but Hartnett was given most of the credit for its modest success. A writer for *WWD* noted that his "knack for projecting authenticity" made a film that might otherwise have come across as absurd seem both humorous and believable. And the *Virginia Pilot* claimed that "the comedy works" because "Hartnett plays his role with earnestness. If Adam Sandler had been cast instead, this would have been a fiasco. Hartnett is hilarious."

Black Hawk Down

Hartnett's personal favorite among all of his films is *Black Hawk Down,* which was released in 2002. Directed by Ridley Scott and produced by Jerry Bruckheimer, who also produced *Pearl Harbor,* it is based on a bestselling true-life story by journalist Mark Bowden. *Black Hawk Down* follows a group of American soldiers who take part in a disastrous mission to capture members of a rebel clan in Mogadishu, Somalia. The doomed mission, which took place in 1993, resulted in the deaths of 18 American soldiers and more than 500 Somalis.

Hartnett played Matt Eversmann, a U.S. Army Ranger who takes part in what is supposed to be a swift and efficient military action. The mission is intended to stop the activities of a Somali warlord who is stealing the food and supplies that are intended for his starving countrymen. The warlord has also killed 24 members of the United Nations peacekeeping force in the area. When the Rangers arrive on the scene, they quickly find themselves trapped in a deadly fight for their lives on the city's rubble-strewn streets. Attempts to rescue them fail when two Black Hawk helicopters are shot down. The chaotic 15-hour battle ends with three dead American soldiers being dragged through the streets of Mogadishu. The movie included a re-creation of this event, which aired repeatedly around the world on television news networks.

—— " ——

Working on Black Hawk Down *gave Hartnett greater respect for members of the military. "[The U.S. soldiers] put themselves in situations where it's life or death, and they've got to make these huge moral decisions that I would never want to have to make," Hartnett said. "Hopefully, when a movie like this comes out, people will think twice about sending our troops on the ground into a land that we don't know anything about, to be slaughtered."*

—— " ——

Promotional posters for Black Hawk Down *emphasized Hartnett's starring role.*

Black Hawk Down focused on telling the story exactly as it occurred, without taking sides or trying to be patriotic. While shooting the film in Morocco, Hartnett met several of the soldiers who actually participated in the ill-fated military operation. The experience gave Hartnett even greater respect for members of the military, but it also increased his doubts about how the United States sometimes chooses to use its military strength. "[The soldiers] put themselves in situations where it's life or death, and they've got to make these huge moral decisions that I would never want to have to make," he commented. "Hopefully, when a movie like this comes out, people will think twice about sending our troops on the ground into a land that we don't know anything about, to be slaughtered."

Hartnett received star billing for *Black Hawk Down,* which won Academy Awards for both film editing and sound. The movie also received a great deal of critical praise. Writing in *Time,* Richard Schickel claimed that it deserves a place "on the very short list of the unforgettable movies about war and its ineradicable and immeasurable costs." The *Atlanta Journal-Constitution,* meanwhile, described the film as a "stunning depiction of war."

Black Hawk Down featured a large cast, and it was more concerned with showing the terrible battle that unfolded in Mogadishu than with character development. Nonetheless, a number of reviewers singled Hartnett out for delivering a strong performance. The *San Francisco Chronicle,* for example, declared that "Hartnett's beautifully delivered final scene" helped turn *Black Hawk Down* into an "exceptional accomplishment."

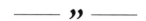

"You get the sense that Josh isn't acting,"says Jerry Bruckheimer, who produced **Pearl Harbor** *and* **Black Hawk Down.** *"With some actors, you see the wheels turning, but not with him. Josh has an inner peace and a strength on screen that bring Gary Cooper to mind."*

After wrapping up the filming of *Black Hawk Down,* Hartnett decided to take some time off. He was upset by the poverty he saw around him while shooting the movie in Morocco. These feelings intensified after the terrorist attacks on the United States of September 11, 2001. The United States responded to the attacks on the World Trade Center and the Pentagon by invading Afghanistan, a Central Asian country where terrorists responsible for the September 11 attacks were believed to be hiding. Hartnett opposed the invasion of Afghanistan, arguing that it mainly hurt innocent people. "Suddenly we hate all these people over there who, most of them, have nothing to do with terrorism and are the innocent victims of our brashness," Hartnett stated. "Suddenly it was us against the world."

*Hartnett, co-star Harrison Ford (left), and director Ron Shelton (center)
on the set of* Hollywood Homicide.

During Hartnett's one-year break from moviemaking, he stated that he wanted to "discover who I am as a person" and to recover from "some important mistakes in my choices," both as an actor and in his personal life. With these goals in mind, he returned to Minnesota to spend time with family and friends.

One year later, Hartnett resumed his acting career by appearing in *Hollywood Homicide*, a comedy about a pair of mismatched police detectives. Hartnett plays K.C. Calden, an easygoing rookie cop who moonlights as a yoga instructor for classes full of beautiful women and aspires to become an actor. Harrison Ford plays his grumpy veteran partner, Joe Gavilan, who sells real estate on the side in order to pay alimony to his many ex-wives. The partners have a number of comic disagreements as they investigate a murder at a rap club. *Hollywood Homicide* received poor reviews upon its release in 2003. *Newsweek* reviewer David Ansen, for example, called it a "numbingly formulaic action comedy" that is "oddly listless from the get-go."

Fame a Mixed Blessing

Now that he is a star and can pick and choose among the scripts that he is offered, Hartnett has vowed to concentrate on "stretching" himself as an actor and finding roles that are unlike those he has already played. He has established his own production company and has agreed to star in an upcoming romantic comedy called *Bob,* about an engaged man who falls in love with an older woman who has children. He has also signed on to star in *Wicker Park,* a psychological drama about a man who is obsessed with the search for a former lover. Reluctant to star in another blockbuster, Hartnett turned down an offer to play Superman in a three-film series. "It didn't feel like the right thing for me," he explained. "Am I going to feel fulfilled doing [the series]? Probably not. It was three films over many months, and I decided that putting on the tights just didn't make sense."

Everyone who has worked with Hartnett comments on his modesty and genuineness. "You get the sense that Josh isn't acting," says Jerry Bruckheimer, who produced *Pearl Harbor* and *Black Hawk Down.* "With some actors, you see the wheels turning, but not with him. Josh has an inner peace and a strength on screen that bring Gary Cooper to mind." Hartnett does not try to attract attention to himself, although he is usually very polite to the fans and autograph-seekers who now dog his every step. "I'm pretty good at returning to life after my work is done," Hartnett said. But he admitted that fame can be a mixed blessing. "It's made it a lot easier to get good projects coming around. I was getting good scripts before but we couldn't get them made into movies because it wasn't commercially viable and so that's changing," he says. "But I've got people sitting in their cars and looking in my windows in front of my house, and that's a little weird."

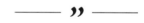

> *"I'm pretty good at returning to life after my work is done," Hartnett said. But he admits that fame can be a mixed blessing. "I've got people sitting in their cars and looking in my windows in front of my house, and that's a little weird."*

HOME AND FAMILY

Hartnett recently bought a house in Minneapolis, where he can be near his family and escape the trappings of Hollywood. "It's one of those ideal places to raise a family," he explained. "It's safe, it's beautiful, there are lakes and cabins." He often stops in to see shows at the Youth Performance

Company, where he got his start in theater. His girlfriend, Ellen Fenster—whom he describes as "a normal person" he would rather keep out of the limelight—is a Minneapolis theater director. He likes to get together and jam with his father, a former guitarist, and his younger siblings, all of whom play musical instruments.

Hartnett describes his family as a group of "very intelligent people who see things for what they are at all times. . . . My family doesn't have to try too hard to maintain balance. It's just natural for them to be able to pick out the BS and choose not to deal with it." Although he occasionally thinks about moving to New York City, Hartnett appreciates the fact that "people in Minneapolis have been very good, extremely polite and reserved. As long as it stays that way, it is my home."

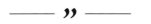

> *Hartnett describes his family as a group of "very intelligent people who see things for what they are at all times. . . . My family doesn't have to try too hard to maintain balance. It's just natural for them to be able to pick out the BS and choose not to deal with it."*

FAVORITE BOOKS AND MOVIES

Hartnett is a big fan of the Beat writers (a group of novelists and poets whose work was popular in the 1950s). In fact, he claims that Jack Kerouac's classic novel *On the Road* changed his life. "It gave me this wanderlust," he recalled. "It made me want to move." One of the highlights of his life was when Lawrence Ferlinghetti, another Beat author, visited the set of *40 Days and 40 Nights* in San Francisco. "I can't even tell you how cool that was," he said.

Trainspotting remains one of his favorite movies. He first saw it when he was a high school student working in a video store. "You see that kind of work and you want to be part of it," he said. Two of the film's stars, Ewan McGregor and Ewen Bremner, later appeared with Hartnett in *Black Hawk Down*. Other recent film favorites include *12 Monkeys, The Usual Suspects,* and *Basquiat*, which he described as "beautifully made, beautifully acted. It's so honest, so spot-on and has such a beautiful message on fame."

HOBBIES AND OTHER INTERESTS

Hartnett has always loved to paint. "It relaxes me because it's just me and the canvas and there's no right way or wrong way," he explained. He also enjoys playing sports—especially baseball, basketball, football, and hockey. But his favorite way to spend time when he is not working is to be with his family in St. Paul.

SELECTED CREDITS

Films

Halloween: H20, 1998
The Faculty, 1998
Here on Earth, 2000
Blow Dry, 2001
The Virgin Suicides, 2000
Town & Country, 2001
Pearl Harbor, 2001
O, 2001
Black Hawk Down, 2001
40 Days and 40 Nights, 2002
Hollywood Homicide, 2003

Television Series

"Cracker," 1997-98

FURTHER READING

Books

Contemporary Theatre, Film, and Television, Vol. 29, 2000
Lanum, Lorelei. *Josh Hartnett: American Idol,* 2002

Periodicals

Atlanta Journal-Constitution, Jan. 18, 2002, p.P1
Details, June/July 2003, p.146
Interview, Jan. 1999, p.68; Feb. 2000, p.146
Minneapolis Star-Tribune, June 1, 2003, p.A1; June 13, 2003, p.E11
New York Times, Mar. 17, 2002, p.17
Newsweek, June 23, 2003, p.63
Observer (London), Apr. 21, 2002, p.14
People Weekly, June 11, 2001, p.69
San Francisco Chronicle, Jan. 18, 2002, p.D1
Seventeen, Mar. 2000, p. 189
Teen People, Feb. 1, 2002, p.58

Vancouver (BC) Province, June 8, 2003, p.D3
Vanity Fair, July 2001, p.83
Virginia Pilot, May 2, 2002, p.E4
YM, Feb. 2002, p.69

Online Databases

Biography Resource Center Online, 2003, article from *Contemporary Theatre, Film, and Television,* Vol. 29, 2000

ADDRESS

Josh Hartnett
Iris Burton Agency
8916 Ashcroft Ave.
Los Angeles, CA 90048

Dolores Huerta 1930-

American Labor Leader
Cofounder of the United Farm Workers

BIRTH

Dolores Huerta was born Dolores Fernandez on April 10, 1930, in Dawson, New Mexico. She was the second of three children born to Juan Fernandez, a coal miner and migrant farm worker, and Alicia (Chavez) Fernandez, a waitress and factory worker. Huerta's parents divorced when she was five years old, and her mother eventually became a restaurant owner and hotel manager. Huerta has two brothers, Juan and Marshall, as well as two much younger half-sisters from her mother's later marriages.

YOUTH

Huerta was born at the beginning of the Great Depression, a time of great economic hardship for many Americans. The tough economic conditions made it tremendously difficult for Alicia Fernandez to support her three children after the divorce. She moved them first to Las Vegas, New Mexico, and then to Stockton, California, a city located in a vast farming region known as the San Joaquin Valley. Hernandez maintained an exhausting schedule to support her children, working as a waitress during the day and toiling in a cannery at night. Huerta and her brothers, meanwhile, took care of laundry and other housecleaning chores under the supervision of their widowed grandfather. His nickname for Huerta was "seven tongues" because she was so talkative. "[My grandfather's] influence was really the male influence in my family," she recalled.

> *Huerta and her brothers took care of household chores under the supervision of their widowed grandfather. "[My grandfather's] influence was really the male influence in my family," she recalled.*

As Huerta grew older, her mother remarried and had another daughter. Alicia Fernandez and her new husband bought a restaurant and a small hotel, where farm workers and their families often stayed. Huerta and her brothers worked there during their summer vacations. During this time, they met many Mexican *braceros* — day laborers who had been hired to work on the valley's fruit and vegetable farms because so many American men were off fighting in World War II. The *braceros* were paid less than regular workers, and Alicia Fernandez often let them stay at her hotel for free. During these summers, young Dolores also came to known and appreciate members of Stockton's other ethnic groups, including Chinese, Japanese, Filipino and Jewish people.

By the early 1950s, Alicia Fernandez had skillfully built the hotel into a successful business enterprise. She divorced her second husband around this time and married Juan Silva, with whom she had another daughter. During this time, she encouraged her eldest daughter to participate in a wide range of activities. Huerta recalled that she pleased her "motivated and ambitious" mother by taking piano, violin, and dancing lessons, singing in the church choir, and serving as a Girl Scout for many years.

Even as a young woman, Huerta was heavily involved in campaigns to improve the lives of migrant farmworkers.

Huerta did not see her father very often when she was growing up, but she never lost contact with him entirely. Her father divided his time between laboring in local coal mines and traveling throughout the American West to harvest crops on big farms. During his travels, he and many other

Mexican-Americans—the primary ethnic group involved in migrant farm work—often endured terrible working conditions. They were paid very low wages for hours of difficult, physically draining labor in the hot sun. Work breaks were often nonexistent, and laborers often had to handle crops that had been treated with pesticides. This constant exposure to pesticides placed their health at significant risk. Working conditions were poor in many other ways as well. For example, many farms did not provide outdoor toilets for workers to use, so workers were forced to suffer the humiliation of squatting down in the fields or hiding behind bushes. The nature of migrant farm labor also forced migrant families to spend much of their

Defining Ethnic Heritage in the Latin American Community

Many different terms are used to define ethnic heritage in the Latin American community. The terms *Chicano* (masculine—pronounced chi-KAHN-oh or shi-KAHN-oh) and *Chicana* (feminine) refer to a person who comes from Mexico or is of Mexican descent. The term comes from the Mexican Spanish word *mexicano,* meaning 'Mexican.' A person of Mexican descent who is a resident or citizen of the United States is often referred to as a *Mexican-American*.

The terms *Latino* (masculine—pronounced la-TEEN-oh) and *Latina* (feminine) refer to a person of Latin-American descent who is living in the United States. Latin America includes all of Mexico as well as other Central and South American countries where Spanish or Portuguese is the national language.

The term *Hispanic,* from the Latin word for "Spain," refers to a person living in the U.S. from any of the countries in either the Northern or Southern hemisphere where Spanish is the primary language. A native of Spain, for example, is a Hispanic but not a Latino.

Although the U.S. government uses the broadest term, *Hispanic,* when referring to members of the Spanish-speaking community, some people find the term offensive. It doesn't sound as Spanish or as culturally authentic as *Latino,* and it doesn't have a feminine form like *Latina*.

To make matters even more confusing, certain terms are preferred in certain parts of the country. For example, *Latino* is used widely in California, while *Hispanic* is more common in Florida and Texas. But even in these states, it is not unusual to find the two terms used interchangeably.

time traveling from farm to farm as various crops became ready for harvest. As a result, migrant workers and their children spent many nights sleeping in their cars or in shacks without heat, plumbing, or running water. Worst of all, young children often ended up working all day alongside their parents because it was the only way the family could earn enough money to survive.

These awful living conditions led Juan Fernandez to become an active participant in labor union activity. Labor unions are organizations formed by workers to protect their rights and interests against unfair or dangerous business practices. In the 1930s he formally joined the local chapter of a union known as the Congress of Industrial Organizations. His union activities eventually brought him into the world of politics. In 1938 he was elected to the New Mexico state legislature, where he worked hard to pass laws that would help migrant workers. He was voted out of office after only one term.

After losing his seat in the legislature, Fernandez worked for a time as a traveling salesman. At age 11, Huerta even spent most of one summer accompanying him on his travels. He eventually moved to Stockton and became a union activist. During this period, he visited his children much more regularly. Looking back, Huerta has expressed pride in her father's efforts on behalf of migrant farmers and other workers. But she also notes that her father held very chauvinistic attitudes toward women. She believes that her father's conviction that men are superior to women was typical of most Chicano (see box) men of his generation.

EDUCATION

Huerta attended Lafayette Grammar School, Jackson Junior High, and Stockton High School. She was a popular student who participated in a variety of extracurricular activities. During her high school years, however, she also experienced several disillusioning instances in which she was the victim of racial prejudice. On one occasion, for example, she organized a teen center that attracted young people from many different ethnic backgrounds. But local police did not like the idea of white teenagers socializing with Chicanos and other minorities, so they closed the center down. Dolores also recalled that she sold more war bonds than anyone else in a school-sponsored contest, but she never received the trophy that had been promised to the winner. She contended that school officials wanted to ignore the contest results because they were embarrassed that a Mexican-American student had out-performed everyone else. "If you were black or brown," she concluded, "you got treated differently."

Huerta walks with Senator Robert F. Kennedy (left) during a 1968 UFW rally.

During the 1940s and 1950s, few Hispanic women were able to go to college. When Huerta graduated from high school in 1948, however, her mother's success as a hotel owner made it possible for her to continue her education. Dolores enrolled at Stockton College, but dropped out before earning her degree to marry her high school boyfriend. They had two children, but the marriage only lasted three years before it ended in divorce. Dolores then returned to Stockton College — now affiliated with University of the Pacific and known as Delta Community College — in the early 1950s. She earned an associate's degree with a certificate in teaching in 1953.

FIRST JOBS

Dolores held a number of jobs in Stockton before she graduated from college. She worked in her mother's hotel during the summers and managed a small grocery store owned by her mother. When the store went out of business, she worked as a secretary at the local U.S. Navy supply base and at the sheriff's office.

After receiving her teaching certificate, Dolores became an elementary school teacher in Stockton. Many of her students came from poor families that supported themselves through migrant farm labor. The sight of barefoot, malnourished children crowding into her classroom every day finally became too much for her to take. She decided to quit her teaching job and get more directly involved in helping farm workers fight poverty. "It just hit me that I could do more by organizing farm workers than by trying to teach their hungry children," she explained.

CAREER HIGHLIGHTS

Becoming a Labor Activist

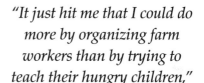

"It just hit me that I could do more by organizing farm workers than by trying to teach their hungry children," Huerta said.

During the 1950s, many minorities in the United States began to challenge the discriminatory practices that existed in nearly every aspect of American society. This dissatisfaction brought about the civil rights movement, which eliminated many laws that discriminated against black Americans and other minorities. During this same period, labor unions delivered higher wages and safer workplace rules for their members. But many migrant farm workers were left behind by these trends. For example, the Fair Labor Standards Act of 1938 established a minimum wage for workers and placed limitations on the amount of overtime a company could demand of its workers. But the law did not cover agricultural workers, most of whom were minorities. Similarly, the National Labor Relations Act of 1935 gave most American workers the right to join or form labor unions and to bargain collectively (as a group) with their employers for decent wages and working conditions. But this law excluded farm workers as well.

Determined to improve the lives of poor migrant families, Huerta decided to work as a volunteer for the Community Service Organization (CSO). This Mexican-American self-help group provided civic and educational programs for Hispanic-Americans, including citizenship classes and voter registration drives. It also pressured local communities with high Hispanic populations to hire more Hispanic police officers and to provide Spanish-speaking people in hospitals, community centers, and government offices so that Mexican-Americans could be guaranteed the same services that white people received. The CSO also encouraged Hispanic-Americans to bring about changes in their schools and their communities by organizing group actions that would draw attention to their needs.

In 1955 Huerta helped establish a CSO chapter in Stockton. She hoped the organization could help the Chicanos and other minority farm workers who came to the San Joaquin Valley every year to harvest crops. As the months passed by, she also launched voter registration drives and publicized incidents in which migrant workers were mistreated by employers, police, and city officials. Over time, Huerta became so skillful at lobbying local government officials on behalf of migrant workers that the CSO hired her as a full-time lobbyist for the organization. As a result, she spent much of her time in the state capital of Sacramento, urging lawmakers to pass laws that would benefit Mexican-Americans.

—— " ——

"[The grape boycott] was like a war," recalled Huerta. "We never slept. We'd get up at 3 or 4 a.m. and then we'd go till 11 p.m. because we'd always have a meeting."

—— " ——

In 1960 Huerta founded an organization known as the Agricultural Workers Association (AWA). Over the next two years, Huerta and the AWA helped persuade California lawmakers to pass more than a dozen laws giving non-citizen workers retirement benefits, medical and disability insurance, and financial support for their families when they were unemployed. Legislators even passed laws that allowed migrant workers to vote and to take their driver's license exams in Spanish.

A Union for Farm Workers

During Huerta's employment at CSO, she also established a strong working relationship with a man named Cesar Chavez. (For more information on Chavez, see *Biography Today,* September 1993.) A former migrant farm worker himself, Chavez had joined the CSO in 1953. By the late 1950s he had gained a reputation as a tireless worker who was determined to improve the lives of the migrant families toiling on the farms of the American West.

In the late 1950s Chavez and Huerta repeatedly tried to persuade the CSO to devote more attention to rural field workers. But the CSO leadership continued to focus most of its efforts on improving the lives of Mexican-Americans located in cities. As a result, Chavez and Huerta left the organization. They moved to Delano, California, where they founded a farm workers' union called the National Farm Workers Association (NFWA) in 1962.

Huerta carries campaign literature during the UFW's grape pickers' strike.

In the beginning, convincing migrant farm workers to join the NFWA was a difficult task. In many instances, their *patrones* (employers) had threatened to fire them and send them back to Mexico if they attended union meetings. Some farm workers had been beaten for trying to join unions, and many were afraid they would be killed. But by visiting the workers in the fields and talking to them face-to-face about what the NFWA could do

67

for them, Chavez and Huerta eventually won their trust. The NFWA gradually became one of the country's most popular organizations for Mexican-Americans.

As time passed, it became clear that Huerta and Chavez were a good team. Chavez possessed a vibrant personality and strong leadership qualities that inspired many workers to join the union. Huerta, meanwhile, excelled as an organizer and negotiator. Time after time, she sat down with fruit and vegetable growers and convinced them to sign contracts in which they promised to provide decent wages and housing for their workers. "I think we really built on each other's strengths," Huerta recalled.

As the NFWA increased in size, it launched several successful lobbying campaigns to improve the lives of its membership. For example, the union urged lawmakers to raise the minimum wage for farm workers. It also worked to establish a credit union and an insurance program for migrant workers, and to allow them to bargain collectively with their employers. The NFWA's lobbying activities also helped convince lawmakers to eliminate a federal law that allowed growers to hire Mexican migrant workers for less money than they paid their American workers.

The Table Grape Boycott

In 1965 Filipino grape pickers who were members of a labor union called the Agricultural Workers Organizing Committee (AWOC) in Delano walked off the job. They declared that they would not return until the growers who employed them raised their wages and contributed to the union's health and welfare fund. This action — called a strike — attracted the support of the NFWA. Led by Chavez and Huerta, the NFWA members joined the strike, boosting the total number of protesting workers to more than 5,000.

Initially, the grape growers who employed the pickers reacted angrily. They used violence and threats in an effort to frighten the workers into ending their strike. But the unions did not back down. Instead, they launched a nationwide table grape boycott — an effort to convince grocery stores and consumers to stop buying grapes that had been grown in California and harvested by underpaid migrant workers. Huerta was the boycott's main organizer. She traveled around the country, raising money to help the strikers and participating in protests designed to draw attention to strikers' demands. In New York, for example, Huerta and various supporters of the boycott — including students, political activists, community and religious groups, and consumers from many different races—picketed in front of grocery stores that sold table grapes until they agreed to take the grapes off the shelves. "It was like a war," Huerta recalled. "We never slept. We'd get up at 3 or 4 a.m. and then we'd go till 11 p.m. because we'd always have a meeting."

In 1966 the AWOC and the NFWA merged to form the United Farm Workers (UFW). That same year Huerta negotiated a new labor contract with Schenley Industries, one of California's grape growing businesses. This contract was a major triumph, for it marked the first time that an agricultural employer had negotiated a collective bargaining agreement with its workers. "Women are particularly good negotiators because we have a lot of patience and no big ego trips to overcome," Huerta later commented. "It unnerves the growers to negotiate with us."

Unfortunately, the other growers did not immediately follow Schenley's lead. The UFW engaged in five more years of strikes and boycotts before the other Delano growers agreed to bargain with union representatives. The resulting contracts gave grape pickers fairer wages, established vacation and holiday pay, and included measures for companies to contribute to the union's health and welfare fund.

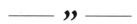

> "[Cesar Chavez and I] always worked as a team, but we used to argue a lot," Huerta admitted. "We had different thoughts on strategies. . . . Sometimes he would win, and sometimes I would win."

The UFW launched other boycotts in the 1970s and 1980s in an effort to improve the lives of its membership. In 1975, for example, a UFW boycott of grapes, lettuce, and Gallo wines was so successful that it led to the passage of the Agricultural Labor Relations Act (ALRA) in California. This law—the first of its kind—forced growers to acknowledge farm workers' right to meet with union organizers. It also forced growers to recognize whatever union the workers chose to represent them.

Huerta and Chavez worked closely together to coordinate these boycotts, but their relationship was a fiery one. "We always worked as a team," she explained, "but we used to argue a lot. We had different thoughts on strategies. . . . Sometimes he would win, and sometimes I would win." On several occasions, Chavez became so angry with Huerta that he fired her. But she always returned to her job within a day or two, and they would start working together again as if nothing had happened.

Huerta and Cesar Chavez (right) were a formidable team for the UFW. They are pictured here with posters of Robert F. Kennedy and Mahatma Gandhi.

Victories for the UFW

By the late 1970s Huerta was in charge of all the UFW's political activities. She spent much of the next several years lobbying Congress to pass a federal law giving amnesty (freedom from punishment) to more than a million illegal immigrants who lived, worked, and paid taxes in the United States but had never become citizens. After years of hard work, the Immigration Act of 1985 was finally passed into law. Years later, Huerta described the act as one of the UFW's most important achievements.

Huerta continued to travel back and forth across the country throughout the 1980s. During this time, she helped establish a United Farm Workers radio station, KUFW-Radio Campesina. In addition, she worked tirelessly to promote Chavez's "Wrath of Grapes" campaign, which focused attention on how pesticides were harming farm workers and their children. "No march is too long, no task too hard for Dolores Huerta if it means taking a step forward for the rights of farm workers," Chavez said. "[She is] totally fearless, both physically and mentally."

The UFW campaign eventually succeeded in forcing growers to stop using pesticides such as DDT and parathion, which had been linked to cancer and birth defects. But the victory was not a total one. Some growers continued to use other chemicals on crops without regard for the potential impact on the health of workers.

"No march is too long, no task too hard for Dolores Huerta if it means taking a step forward for the rights of farm workers," said Chavez. "[She is] totally fearless, both physically and mentally."

In 1988 Huerta traveled to San Francisco, where Vice President George Bush was campaigning for president (he eventually became the 41st president of the United States). She joined a protest that had been organized outside a Bush campaign event. The aim of the protest was to publicize the UFW's boycott activities, highlight its campaign to reduce worker exposure to dangerous agricultural chemicals, and criticize Bush's views on worker issues. But as the protest continued, tensions rose between participants and police officers responsible for controlling the crowd. At one point, Huerta was clubbed by an officer. The injuries forced her to a local hospital, where she had emergency surgery to remove a ruptured spleen and repair several broken ribs.

Huerta speaks at a rally in the 1970s.

Huerta later sued the city for the officer's actions. She eventually received an $825,000 settlement from the city, which also agreed to make changes in the methods its police department used to control large crowds. After recovering from her injuries, Huerta returned to the UFW, where she continued to attend farm workers' rallies, participate in strikes, and negotiate contracts with growers.

Decline of the UFW

Membership in the UFW had peaked at about 100,000 in the 1970s. In the 1980s, however, it underwent a steady decline, dropping to fewer than 40,000 members. Some observers claimed that the UFW was hurt by the conservative, pro-business administration of President Ronald Reagan, who served from January 1981 to January 1989. Others pointed to diminished media coverage of UFW boycotts, which limited their effectiveness. Some critics also claimed that members left because the union failed to bring about major improvements in the lives of farm workers and their families. For example, most farmer workers still earned less than the minimum wage in the early 1990s. It seemed to many people that farm workers had no more money or job security than they'd had before the union came along.

In 1993 the struggling union suffered another serious blow when Cesar Chavez died. "That was one of the saddest days I have ever known," Huerta said. "I think his death was a loss for all mankind. He was a real leader, like Mahatma Ghandi or Martin Luther King, and like them he believed in nonviolence." Chavez's son-in-law, Arturo Rodriguez, became the union's new president, and together he and Huerta worked harder than ever to keep the UFW alive. For example, they devoted a great deal of energy in the mid-1990s to establishing a union presence in the strawberry industry. But in 1996 their efforts were rejected by the strawberry workers. Many of these workers viewed the UFW as "a family business driven by money and power" rather than as an organization that could help them.

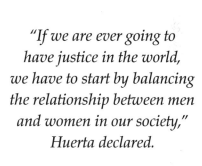

"If we are ever going to have justice in the world, we have to start by balancing the relationship between men and women in our society," *Huerta declared.*

Huerta remained strong in the face of these disappointing events. In fact, she expanded the scope of her activities. In addition to her UFW work, she became heavily involved in specific efforts to improve the lives of Latino women. For example, she helped launch campaigns to eliminate sexual harassment of female farm workers and support the election of women to public office. She also helped found the Coalition of Labor Union Women (CLUW), a group aimed at increasing women's participation in union activities. "If we are ever going to have justice in the world, we have to start by balancing the relationship between men and women in our society," she explained.

Many women were inspired by Huerta's leadership in these areas. "Mexican women used to do what the men said, but Dolores Huerta was our example of something different," said one female union member. "She was always out in front, and she would talk back. She wasn't scared of anything."

Huerta speaks out against cuts in state education funding at a 2003 rally in California.

In the late 1990s, meanwhile, the UFW tried to revitalize itself through a shift in strategy. It placed less emphasis on strikes, which were not always effective and sometimes resulted in violence. Instead, the union's leadership relied more heavily on tactics like Huerta's "Five Cents for Fairness" campaign. Under this strategy, the UFW urged consumers to pay five cents more for a basket of strawberries so that the strawberry pickers could earn higher wages. In addition, the union began to place more emphasis on organizing entire industries instead of individual farm operations.

A Lifelong Crusader

In 1999 Huerta left her position as vice president of the UFW to work for Al Gore's presidential campaign. She was about to leave on a campaign trip through the state of California when she was admitted to the hospital. At first, doctors thought that she was suffering from a bleeding ulcer. They eventually realized, however, that she had a bleeding artery in her intestine. Her condition remained critical for several days as doctors treated her. She then spent the next several months recovering. But even during her recovery, she spent much of her time drawing up plans to establish a leadership foundation that would train young people as community organizers.

In 2002, at the age of 72, Huerta participated in a 165-mile walk through searing temperatures in California's Central Valley to the state capitol at Sacramento. Once she and other demonstrators arrived at the capitol, they urged California Governor Gray Davis to sign a bill that would end a stalemate in negotiations between growers and farm workers. Davis eventually signed the bill, and the new law went into effect in September 2002.

Huerta no longer holds an active position in the union, but she continues to promote its causes in her usual energetic fashion. In recent years she assisted in the establishment of a retirement village for farm workers. She also helped pass a ban on the use of short-handled hoes for harvesting, because the use of these tools often caused serious back problems for pickers. In addition, she helped agricultural workers gain greater access to medical insurance, pensions, educational funds, vacation and overtime pay, and other benefits. "My vision is for the farm workers to have the same rights, protection, and wages that other workers in this country have," she explained. "As long as my health holds out I want to pass my experiences along to help other people."

Huerta thinks that the UFW's nonviolent approach to confrontations with growers has been its most enduring contribution. "I think we brought to the world, the United States anyway, the whole idea of boycotting as a nonviolent tactic. I think we showed the world that nonviolence can work to make social change. . . . I think we have laid a pattern of how farm workers are eventually going to get out of their bondage."

———— **"** ————

"I think we brought to the world, the United States anyway, the whole idea of boycotting as a nonviolent tactic,"Huerta said."I think we showed the world that nonviolence can work to make social change. . . . I think we laid a pattern of how farm workers are eventually going to get out of their bondage."

———— **"** ————
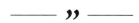

MARRIAGE AND FAMILY

Huerta married Ralph Head when she was a college student. They had two daughters—Celeste and Lori—before their marriage ended after three years. She later married her second husband, Ventura Huerta, and had five children—Fidel, Emilio, Vincent, Alicia, and Angela. Their marriage fell apart when it became clear, in Dolores's words, "that I cared more about helping other people than cleaning our house and doing my hair." In the early 1970s Huerta became romantically involved with Richard Chavez, Cesar Chavez's brother. Although they never married, they had four children together—Juanita, Maria Elena, Ricardo, and Camilla—and their relationship continues today.

Huerta, who lives in Bakersfield, California, admits that her 11 children have had to make sacrifices because of her UFW work. For many years they depended on donations for their food and clothing, and their mother's hectic travel schedule forced them to spend long periods living with friends or moving from school to school. Her daughter Lori says, "I remember, as a child, one time talking to her about my sadness that she wasn't going to be with me on my birthday. And she said that the sacrifices we as her children make would help hundreds of other children in the future. How can you argue with something like that?"

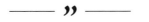

> "I don't feel proud of the suffering that my kids went through. I feel very bad and guilty about it, but by the same token I know that they learned a lot in the process."

For her part, Huerta admits that her kids endured difficult childhoods. "I don't feel proud of the suffering that my kids went through," she said. "I feel very bad and guilty about it, but by the same token I know that they learned a lot in the process." She believes that her children, several of whom have inherited their mother's devotion to activism, are better off as adults because of the values their mother instilled in them. "I expect them to follow their dreams, to change the world, to make the world a better place," she says.

HONORS AND AWARDS

Outstanding Labor Leader Award (California State Senate): 1984
National Women's Hall of Fame: 1993
Outstanding American Award (Eugene V. Debs Foundation): 1993
Roger Baldwin Award (American Civil Liberties Union): 1993
Ellis Island Medal of Freedom Award (National Ethnic Coalition of
    Organizations): 1993
Earl Warren Civil Liberties Award (American Civil Liberties Union): 1996
Eleanor Roosevelt Human Rights Award (U.S. Government): 1999

Hispanic Heritage Award: 2000
Puffin/Nation Prize for Creative Citizenship (Puffin Foundation and
    Nation Institute): 2002

FURTHER READING

Books

Latinas! Women of Achievement, 1996

Periodicals

Hispanic, Aug. 1996, p.41
Latino Leaders, Feb.-Mar. 2000, p.49
Los Angeles Times, Apr. 29, 1999, Metro section p.1; Aug. 15, 1999, p.NA
Minneapolis Star Tribune, May 16, 1995, p. D1
Ms., Nov. 1976, p.11; Jan.-Feb. 1998, p.46
The Nation, Feb. 23, 1974, p.232; Dec. 23, 2002, p.7

Online Articles

http://www.latinoleaders.com
    (*Latino Leaders,* "Dolores Huerta: Secretary-Treasurer/United Farm
    Workers of America," Feb.- Mar. 2000)
http://www.hispaniconline.com
    (*Hispaniconline.com,* "For the Sake of Good: Civil Rights Activist Dolores
    Huerta Proves that Ordinary People Can Stand Up for Justice — and
    Win," May 2003)

ADDRESS

Dolores Huerta
United Farm Workers of America
P. O. Box 62
Keene, CA 93531

WORLD WIDE WEB SITES

http://www.ufw.org/
http://www.nwhp.org/

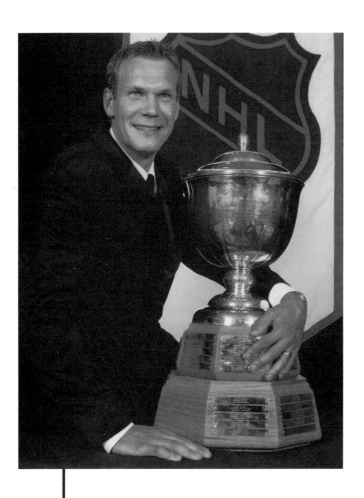

Nicklas Lidstrom 1970-

Swedish Professional Hockey Player for the Detroit
Red Wings
Three-Time Winner of the Norris Trophy as the NHL's
Best Defenseman

BIRTH

Nicklas Lidstrom was born on April 28, 1970, in Vasteras, Sweden, a city located about 60 miles from the national capital of
Stockholm. His father, Jan-Eric Lidstrom, worked as an engi-
neer for the Swedish highway system. His mother's name is
Gerd.

YOUTH AND EDUCATION

Lidstrom was raised in Avesta, a town near Vasteras. His father claims that Lidstrom was a spirited and outgoing boy. "He was a little warrior, always joking and doing little things to get into trouble," Jan-Eric Lidstrom recalled. But Lidstrom has described himself as a more laid-back youngster. "I've always been quiet," he said. "Ever since I was a little kid, I've always been quiet."

As was the case in most other Swedish communities, many children in Avesta played ice hockey at an early age. By the time Lidstrom started playing hockey at age 7, he recalled that "all the kids where I lived were already playing hockey. . . . It was natural for me to get involved." Within a few months of lacing up his skates, he was one of the top players in his age group in all of Avesta.

Lidstrom enjoyed other sports, too, of course. For example, he displayed top soccer skills at an early age. But hockey gradually emerged as his favorite. He spent hours competing in youth leagues and in pick-up games at local rinks. "When I first started out, I just wanted to play on the big team in my hometown," he recalled. "When I was 13 or 14, I wanted to play in the Elite league [the top pro hockey league in Sweden]. It wasn't until I was about 16 that I started to think about the NHL." Indeed, Lidstrom spent many evenings watching broadcasts of National Hockey League (NHL) games. He especially enjoyed watching the Toronto Maple Leafs, which featured Borje Salming, one of the first Swedish players ever to play in the NHL. "He was a hero, for sure," remembered Lidstrom. "My idol."

Lidstrom attended school in Avesta as well. In the Swedish school system, all students start learning the English language at age 10. As a result, he became proficient in English by his mid-teens. Years later, when he became a player in the NHL, his mastery of the English language made it much easier for him to make the transition to living in the United States.

CAREER HIGHLIGHTS

From Sweden to Detroit

By his late teens, Lidstrom was one of Sweden's most promising young hockey players. Even in Sweden's elite competitive leagues, his all-around abilities attracted notice. Before long, the talented young defenseman was playing in front of crowds that included NHL scouts from the United States and Canada.

Lidstrom carries the puck down the ice in a 1997 game.

In 1989 the NHL's Detroit Red Wings selected Lidstrom in the third round of the league draft with the 53rd selection overall. Jimmy Devellano, who was the club's general manager in 1989, later admitted that he drafted the young Swedish player without ever seeing him play. "You have to believe in your scouts, and that's what we were doing," he explained. "You have to understand, we're drafting kids 17, 18 years old. All you're doing is projecting how they will develop. You do the best you can do, evaluating them. But you never know."

Lidstrom was delighted that the Red Wings drafted him. "The NHL seemed so far away," he said. "You read and heard about the players, but you never imagined you'd be part of it. I wanted to see what it was like." But instead of leaving immediately for the NHL, Lidstrom stayed in Sweden to play hockey for the next two years. This decision met with the approval of the Red Wings organization. Detroit's staff knew that the young Swede would have the opportunity to play a lot of hockey in his homeland, but that he would get only limited playing time in the ultra-competitive NHL.

Lidstrom spent the 1990 and 1991 seasons playing for Vasteras in the Swedish Elite League. He also helped Team Sweden win a gold medal at the 1991 World Championship. These experiences allowed him to hone his defensive skills against star players from Sweden and other countries. "I was glad that I waited a couple of years after I was drafted to come to the NHL," he later admitted. "I was more confident. Playing at the World Championships in 1991 against NHL players also helped my confidence."

"When I first started out, I just wanted to play on the big team in my hometown," Lidstrom recalled. *"It wasn't until I was about 16 that I started to think about the NHL."*

Lidstrom finally joined the Red Wings for the 1991-92 season. "When I first came over, I thought I might stay two or three years," he said. "I just wanted to see if I could play at this level." As it turned out, the young defenseman made an immediate impact. Impressed by his smart and steady play, Red Wings coaches gave him lots of "ice time" — playing time — from the very first game. By the end of the season, Lidstrom had earned a spot on the NHL All-Rookie Team. He also finished second to rookie sensation Pavel Bure in the balloting for the Calder Trophy, given each season to the league's top first-year player. In addition, Lidstrom helped Detroit post a 43-25-12 (43 wins, 25 losses, 12 ties) record and a first-place finish in their division. "Just the way he stepped in and played right away, the ability he showed, you knew he had a chance to be a special player," recalled Devellano. "He helped us a lot that season."

After the season was over, Lidstrom admitted that the year had taken a lot out of him. "When I first came over here, I didn't know anything," he explained. "How to order a phone, find an apartment, things like that." In addition, he said that the NHL's 82-game regular season was "definitely an adjustment. We'd play 40 games in the regular season [back in Sweden], and there were many breaks. We'd get almost three weeks off for Christmas, and breaks before the national tournament. Just a lot of time off. The NHL isn't like that."

Developing into a Quiet Star

Over the next several seasons, Lidstrom developed into one of the most important players on the Wings. His playmaking abilities and sound defensive skills contributed to Detroit's emergence as one of the NHL's most dangerous teams. Indeed, from 1992-93 to 1995-96, the Red Wings earned three division titles and two President's Trophies, given each year to the NHL team with the best regular season record. But in each of these seasons, the club fell short in its bid to win the Stanley Cup as NHL champions.

> "*It's refreshing to see an athlete who's just down-to-earth,"said one of Lidstrom's teammates. "Somebody that doesn't think the world owes him something. Some people like to be in the limelight, they want to be on TV every day. Other people are happy sitting in the shadows, being their own man. I'm sure he'd love to get the recognition that he deserves. But you're not going to see him go out and pound the drums for it."*

Lidstrom's teammates recognized that he was an important factor in the team's success. Outside of Detroit, however, the defensive ace received little recognition. "He always seems to be the forgotten guy," said fellow Red Wing Darren McCarty. "We were perfectly happy to keep him a sleeper."

Many of Lidstrom's teammates attributed his low public profile to his refusal to seek out publicity. "It's refreshing to see an athlete who's just down-to-earth," said teammate Mike Ramsay. "Somebody that doesn't think the world owes him something. Some people like to be in the limelight, they want to be on TV every day. Other people are happy sitting in the shadows, being their own man. I'm sure he'd love to get the recognition that he deserves. But you're not going to see him go out and pound the drums for it." For his part, Lidstrom simply observed that "I'm pretty calm and quiet. I don't really avoid attention, but I don't look for it either, in the locker room or on the ice."

Winning the Stanley Cup

As the 1996-97 season unfolded, Lidstrom took his game to a new level. In addition to playing his usual flawless defense, he used his skating, shooting, and puckhandling skills to give Detroit another major scoring threat.

During the 1990s Lidstrom emerged as one of the league's best defensemen.

Many of his goals and assists came on the Wings' power play. (In hockey, players who commit penalties must leave the ice for a set period of time. That gives the opposing team a "power play" in which they can attack with an extra skater on the ice.) "All through my career I've been used on the power play," Lidstrom said. "I have to play a solid game overall and play well defensively, but I think people expect me to play well offensively, especially on the power play."

By the end of the regular season, Lidstrom's 57 points (15 goals, 42 assists) ranked third among all NHL defensemen. These totals—along with his smothering defense—helped boost Detroit to a 38-26-18 record and another playoff berth. The quiet Swede excelled in the playoffs as well, as the Wings marched to a spot in the 1997 Stanley Cup finals against the Philadelphia Flyers. The Red Wings overwhelmed the Flyers in four straight games to clinch the club's first NHL championship in 42 years.

Many Red Wings played important roles in the team's championship drive, but hockey experts claimed that Lidstrom was particularly valuable. For example, Head Coach Scotty Bowman often used Lidstrom against Philadelphia superstar Eric Lindros during the finals. Other teams had failed to contain Lindros, one of the league's biggest and strongest players. But Lidstrom used his smarts and skating ability to thoroughly neutralize the bigger man's game. "We like to have him out there against the other team's top offensive line," Bowman acknowledged. "His main job is to prevent goals, not to score them. He's very underrated defensively."

Stardom Finally Arrives

Lidstrom maintained his excellent standard of play during the 1997-98 season. He finished second on the team in points (with 59 points, including 17 goals and 42 assists) and led the entire league in scoring by a defenseman. He also made his second straight appearance in the NHL All-Star Game, and finished second in the voting for the Norris Trophy, given each year to the league's best defenseman. Most important, he helped the Red Wings clinch a second straight Stanley Cup. The team posted a 44-23-14 record in the regular season, then marched through the playoffs to claim another championship. During Detroit's playoff run, Lidstrom set team records for most assists (13) and points (19) by a defenseman in a single playoff year.

"Nick plays more quality minutes than maybe anyone in the NHL," said Steve Yzerman. "He kills penalties, plays on our power play, and he's always out there on defense against the opposing team's best players. I'd hate to have to find out just how ordinary we'd be without him."

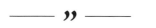

The 1998-99 season came to a disappointing close for Lidstrom. The team posted a 43-27-7 record and clinched another division title, but it failed in its quest to win a third straight Stanley Cup. Still, Lidstrom could take comfort in the fact that he emerged as a true NHL star during the course of the season. He was voted to start in the NHL All-Star Game for the first time, and praise for his mistake-free style poured in from all corners of the league. "Lidstrom's game is fueled by his incredible hockey sense," wrote analyst Karl Samuelson for NHL.com. "An excellent skater with tremendous vision on the ice, the talented defenseman has an effortless way of accomplishing his dominance on the blue line. Lidstrom does not crush his opponents through the glass . . . nor does he try to skate through the other team. Instead, he establishes his superiority in an understated manner."

At season's end, Lidstrom once again finished second in the voting for the Norris Trophy. He also finished second in the voting to Wayne Gretzky for the Lady Byng Trophy, which is awarded to the player who exhibits the

Lidstrom uses skating ability and positioning to collar opposing players.

best sportsmanship. Many of Lidstrom's teammates expressed deep satisfaction with the belated recognition. "Nick plays more quality minutes than maybe anyone in the NHL," said teammate Steve Yzerman. "He kills penalties, plays on our power play, and he's always out there on defense against the opposing team's best players. I'd hate to have to find out just how ordinary we'd be without him."

Considering a Return to Sweden

In the summer of 1999, Lidstrom shocked Detroit hockey fans with an announcement that he was thinking about leaving the NHL and taking his family back to Sweden. "My family comes first, I've always said that," he said. He noted that he liked living in the Detroit area, but that his closest friends and family still lived in Sweden. He also wanted to make certain that his children appreciated their Swedish heritage.

———— " ————

"The issue all along has been to do what's best for our kids," Lidstrom said about deciding when to return to Sweden. "What finally made the difference was that we talked to several friends that lived in the States for a time and then returned to Sweden. Like us, they felt it was important to raise their families in Sweden. But they all agreed that there was no problem with their kids living there longer than what we already have."

———— " ————

Over the next several weeks, Lidstrom struggled with the decision. He knew that he could make much more money playing hockey in the United States, but he missed his friends and family. Another important factor to consider was Sweden's shorter hockey season, which would leave him with more time to spend with his family. Ultimately, however, Lidstrom decided to remain with the Red Wings. In September 1999 he agreed to a new contract that paid him $22 million over three years. "The issue all along has been to do what's best for our kids," he said. "What finally made the difference was that we talked to several friends that lived in the States for a time and then returned to Sweden. Like us, they felt it was important to raise their families in Sweden. But they all agreed that there was no problem with their kids living there longer than what we already have."

In the 1999-2000 campaign, Lidstrom maintained his steady standard of excellence. He finished second in the voting for both the Norris Trophy and the Lady Byng Trophy. He also set career bests in several categories, including goals (20), power play goals (9), and power play points (31). In addition, he led all NHL defensemen in points (73) and was named captain of the World Team in the 2000 NHL All-Star Game. The Red Wings, meanwhile, remained one of the league's top teams. They finished the season with a 48-24-10 record and entered the

Lidstrom celebrates winning both the Stanley Cup and the Conn Smythe Trophy as most valuable player of the 2002 NHL Playoffs.

playoffs as a Stanley Cup favorite, only to see the New Jersey Devils claim the title.

In 2000-01, Lidstrom finished second on the Wings in points (71) and set a new career mark for assists (56). His 71 points placed him second among all NHL defensemen in scoring and helped Detroit march to a division-best 49-20-9 mark. As season's end, Lidstrom finally claimed the Norris Trophy as the league's best defenseman, after three straight years of being runner-up. According to Red Wings General Manager Ken Holland, no other player in the NHL was more deserving of the honor. "Nick is a solid all-around player in every aspect of the game," declared Holland. "He can score and is a great passer. Nick knows when to jump into the play and is excellent defensively. He is not overly physical, but doesn't get beat one-on-one because he is so smart. He knows how to position himself and has such quick feet and skating ability that he knows how to adjust to situations. . . . Nick is so smooth in everything he does on the ice. He is almost like silk."

Winning the Conn Smythe Trophy

Lidstrom enjoyed another banner season in 2001-02. He represented Sweden in the 2002 Winter Olympics in Salt Lake City, Utah, and in December 2001 he signed a new contract with Detroit that pays him $10 million a season through 2003-04. By season's end he had tied for the league lead in points by a defenseman (59) and earned his second straight Norris Trophy.

"I was really surprised to win [the Conn Smythe Trophy]," Lidstrom admitted. "It's an honor I'll never forget. . . . I'm not a flashy player, but I do my job out there playing a lot of minutes. It's a tremendous honor to receive this award."

Best of all, the Red Wings claimed the Stanley Cup for the third time in six seasons. Armed with a roster of future Hall of Famers, including Steve Yzerman, Brett Hull, and Dominick Hasek, the Red Wings finished the regular season with an amazing 51-17-10 mark. Detroit then dropped the first two games of the playoffs to the underdog Vancouver Canucks. But Lidstrom scored the winning goal in Game Three, and the Wings dominated the series from that point forward. Detroit then marched to the Western Conference finals, where they knocked off their archrivals, the Colorado Avalanche, in a tense seven-game series. In the Stanley Cup finals, Detroit lost the first game to the Carolina Hurricanes. But in Game Two, Lidstrom delivered another game-winning goal. After punching the puck into the net, he pumped both fist and roared at his ecstatic teammates. "I guess my teammates were surprised I showed emotion," he later said. "It's the old Swedish stereotype [that] I don't get excited, don't show it as much as others."

After tying the series at one game apiece, the Wings went on to win the next three games and claim the Cup. As the Wings celebrated, Lidstrom (5 goals, 11 assists in the playoffs) learned that he had been awarded the Conn Smythe Trophy as the Most Valuable Player of the playoffs. He thus became the first European player, the second non-Canadian, and the seventh defenseman ever to receive the Conn Smythe Trophy. "I was really surprised to win it," he admitted. "I wasn't even thinking about it, really. You want to win the Stanley Cup. But it's an honor I'll never forget. . . . I'm not a flashy player, but I do my job out there playing a lot of minutes. It's a tremendous honor to receive this award."

After winning the 2002 Stanley Cup, Lidstrom's sons Adam (center) and Kevin (right) joined their father on the ice for the post-game celebration.

Lidstrom's teammates were happy for him, too. "He's been our best player for a long time now," claimed Yzerman. "He's a quiet guy, but he's the best guy I've ever played with. You have to watch him closely to appreciate how good he is." Teammate Boyd Devereaux offered similar praise. "He totally deserved it," said Devereaux. "I'm the biggest fan of Nick. He's the greatest guy in the world."

As Lidstrom prepared for the 2002-03 season, he learned that *Hockey News* had ranked him as the best player in the NHL. Lidstrom appreciated the kind words, but he did not let them distract him from his on-ice responsibilities. He performed at his usual high level, and at midseason he was rewarded by fans, who cast more All Star votes for him than any other player in the league. By season's end, Lidstrom had earned his third consecutive Norris Trophy as the league's best defenseman. He also finished second in the voting for the Lady Byng Trophy for the fourth time in five years. "He's like a Swiss watch, always in control," marveled first-year head coach Dave Lewis, who replaced the retiring Scotty Bowman. "He's just such a complete player, so very efficient. You look at the amount of ice time he plays, and the type of level he plays at, it's quite remarkable."

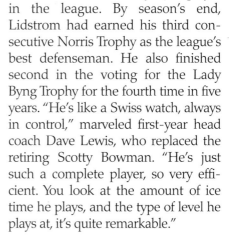

> "He's like a Swiss watch, always in control," said Coach Dave Lewis. "He's just such a complete player, so very efficient. You look at the amount of ice time he plays, and the type of level he plays at, it's quite remarkable."

Unfortunately for the Red Wings, the season ended in bitter disappointment. As the playoffs began, many experts picked Detroit to repeat as NHL champs. Instead, they were swept from the playoffs in the opening round by the Anaheim Mighty Ducks. This loss shocked everyone in the Detroit clubhouse. But despite this setback, analysts, coaches, and players around the league believe that Lidstrom and his teammates will be Stanley Cup contenders for the next several seasons.

MARRIAGE AND FAMILY

Lidstrom and his wife Annika have three sons, Kevin, Adam, and Samuel. During hockey season, the Lidstrom family lives in Novi, Michigan, a suburb of Detroit. They also own a home in Vasteras, Sweden, where they spend the offseason. Lidstrom has repeatedly stated that he intends to move his family to Vasteras permanently after his NHL playing career is over.

HOBBIES AND OTHER INTERESTS

Lidstrom is a big sports fan. He especially enjoys American football. "I enjoy the games and the action," he said. "I've been to a few [Detroit] Lions games. I like sitting in the crowd and watching the games. It's fun."

HONORS AND AWARDS

World Hockey Championship: 1991, gold medal
NHL All-Star: 1996, 1998-2003
NHL First Team All-Star: 1998-2003
World Cup: 1996, as member of Team Sweden
Olympic Hockey: 1998, 2002, as member of Team Sweden
Norris Trophy: 2001-2003, for NHL's best defenseman
Conn Smythe Trophy: 2002, for most valuable player of the playoffs

FURTHER READING

Books

Cotsonika, Nicholas J. *Hockey Gods: The Inside Story of the Red Wings' Hall-of-Fame Team,* 2002
Duff, Bob. *History of Hockeytown: Detroit Red Wings, 75 Years,* 2002
Fischler, Stan. *Detroit Red Wings: Greatest Moments and Players,* 2002
Romanuk, Paul. *Hockey Superstars, 1998-1999,* 1998 (juvenile)

Periodicals

Chicago Tribune, May 7, 1999, p.N1
Denver Post, Apr. 6, 2001, p.D13
Detroit Free Press, Oct. 30, 1991, p.C2; Jan. 19, 1996, p.C5; Apr. 15, 1997, p.D1; June 7, 1997, p.B1; Feb. 24, 1998, p.D1; June 11, 1998, p.D2; Jan. 23, 1999, p.B1; June 14, 2001, p.C7; June 15, 2001, p.D1; Dec. 8, 2001, p.B1
Detroit News, June 15, 2001, p.A1; Jan. 28, 2003, p.1 (Special); June 13, 2003, p.H3
Grand Rapids (Michigan) Press, June 14, 2002, p.B2
New York Times, June 8, 2002, p.D3
Sporting News, Sep. 6, 1999, p.90
Sports Illustrated, June 2, 1997, p.54; June 16, 1997, p.28; Jan. 12, 1998, p.66; Apr. 3, 2000, p.70; June 17, 2002, p.58; June 27, 2002, p.74
Sports Illustrated for Kids, Jan. 1, 2003, p.48
Windsor (Ontario) Star, Feb. 7, 1992, p.B1

Online Articles

http://www.asapsports.com
  (*ASAP Sports Web Site*, "An Interview with Nicklas Lidstrom,"
  June 13, 2002)
http://www.nhl.com
  (*NHL.com*, "Dependable Lidstrom Stands Alone," Jan. 23, 2003;
  "Lidstrom: No Need to Plan Ahead," Jan. 23, 2003; "Lidstrom Plays
  'Swede' Music in Detroit," Jan. 23, 2003)
http://www.washingtonpost.com
  (*Washington Post Online*, "For Wings' Lidstrom, No Place Like Home,"
  June 15, 1998)

Online Databases

Biography Resource Center Online, 2002, reproduced in *Biography Resource
  Center*, 2003

ADDRESS

Nicklas Lidstrom
Detroit Red Wings
Joe Louis Arena
600 Civic Center Drive
Detroit, MI 48226

WORLD WIDE WEB SITES

www.nhl.com
www.nhlpa.com
www.detroitredwings.com

Nelly 1974-

American Rap Artist
Creator of the Chart-Topping CDs *Country Grammar*
and *Nellyville*

BIRTH

Nelly was born Cornell Haynes, Jr., on November 2, 1974, in
Austin, Texas. Nelly's record company, however, has repeatedly claimed that he was born in the late 1970s to make it appear
that he is closer in age to rap music's teenage fan base. His
nickname is actually a shortened version of "Nelly Nel," which
he was called in his youth. Nelly's father is Cornell Haynes,

Sr., who served as a non-commissioned officer in the U.S. Air Force. His mother, Rhonda Mack, worked in fast food restaurants. Nelly's parents divorced when he was seven years old. He is the only offspring of his parents' marriage, but he is believed to have a half-sister and a step-brother.

YOUTH

When Nelly was a small child, he and his mother followed his father on military assignments around the world. They eventually settled in St. Louis, where they lived in a poor neighborhood filled with condemned buildings and empty lots. After his parents divorced, Nelly remained with his mother. But Rhonda Mack became concerned about the influence of older neighborhood boys on her son. In addition, she decided that she could not support her son on the modest wages she earned at fast food restaurants. As a result, she sent him to live with various relatives and friends over the next several years. "I never spent more than three years in one household," Nelly said. "I had to basically raise myself because I was constantly on the move. I learned to depend on myself, which is good, but as a kid you look at it like, 'Why don't nobody want me?'"

> ————— **"** —————
>
> *"I never spent more than three years in one household," Nelly said. "I had to basically raise myself because I was constantly on the move. I learned to depend on myself, which is good, but as a kid you look at it like, 'Why don't nobody want me?'"*
>
> ————— **"** —————

This unsettled existence continued until Nelly's teen years, when his mother managed to find a home for them in University City, a middle-class, integrated suburb of St. Louis near Washington University. Nelly's mother hoped that as her son became accustomed to his new home, he would be less vulnerable to street gangs and other negative influences.

At first, the move to University City seemed to be a positive one for Nelly. He started playing baseball—a game at which he proved to be very talented—and became a big fan of hip-hop and rap artists such as LL Cool J, Run-DMC, Goodie Mob, OutKast, and Jay-Z. He soon discovered that he possessed a gift for rhyming and storytelling, and before long he was spinning out rap songs of his own.

For a while it appeared that Nelly might be headed for a career as a professional baseball player. A star shortstop in the St. Louis Amateur Baseball

Nelly's favorite rap subjects include partying, women, and cars.

Association, his performance caught the attention of a number of major league scouts. He was even invited to training camps held by the Atlanta Braves and the Pittsburgh Pirates. But Nelly lacked the discipline and dedication that the sport required. Instead of focusing on baseball, he became heavily involved in dealing drugs and other illegal activities. "I wanted the cars, I wanted the jewelry. I wanted all that [crap] I didn't really need at the time," Nelly confessed. "So I kind of got out of the baseball thing and went back to the 'hood."

EDUCATION

Nelly attended eight different schools in 12 years. Throughout, his school record was marked by poor grades, fights, and expulsions for disruptive behavior. In fact, he was expelled from four different schools during his youth. "He was a handful," agreed his mother, "but what child isn't?" By the time he reached high school, his studies had taken a back seat to making money. At first, he earned his money honestly by working as a cashier at McDonald's and loading trucks for the United Parcel Service (UPS). But as time passed, he turned to drug dealing and street crimes to put money in his wallet.

As a senior at University City High School in 1993, however, Nelly became involved in a musical venture that changed his life forever. He joined together with Robert "Kyjuan" Cleveland, Tohri "Murphy Lee" Harper, "Big Lee" Ali Jones, Corey "Slo Down" Edwards, and Lavell "City Spud" Webb. Together they formed a rap group called the St. Lunatics, an African-American nickname for "St. Louis." As the weeks passed by, music became a positive outlet for the group's members. In fact, Nelly and the other group members made a vow to each other that they would stay away from illegal activities and focus instead on getting jobs and earning enough money to record their songs.

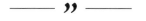

> "We said, yo, let's not talk about killing and robbing," explained one St. Lunatics member. "Let's just talk about partying and having fun, get the whole world — black people, white people — into our music."

At first, the St. Lunatics performed "gangsta' rap," in which inner-city violence and crime are major themes. But when "Big Lee" left the group to attend college, it made the other members think about life beyond the streets of St. Louis. When Big Lee came home to visit, he advised his fellow band members to listen to other rap groups and develop a sound that would set their own music apart. Day after day, Nelly and his friends went to the studio to work on developing their own unique style. They finally decided that instead of performing rap tunes about street life and crime, they would write songs with a more positive message. "We said, yo, let's not talk about killing and robbing," explained Ali Jones. "Let's just talk about partying and having fun, get the whole world — black people, white people — into our music."

CAREER HIGHLIGHTS

Climbing to the Top

In 1996 the St. Lunatics recorded a song called "Gimme What Ya Got" that a local newspaper described as a "a heavy-on-the-bass ditty that challenges rappers to come up with decent lyrics." Nelly and his friends quickly distributed the song to record stores and radio stations around the city. To everyone's surprise, it became the number one tune on the most popular hip-hop station in St. Louis, and it eventually sold 10,000 copies.

Nelly poses with members of the St. Lunatics.

Energized by the success of "Gimme What Ya Got," the St. Lunatics put together another single called "Who's the Boss," which was also a local hit. But despite these successes, the group failed to attract the attention of the big rap record labels. Executives with the major rap record companies seemed to be interested only in rap artists based in New York, Los Angeles, and other major cities on the East and West Coasts. The group decided that its best bet for success was for Nelly, who had the rhyming skills and stage presence to sell himself as a solo artist, to seek a recording contract on his own. If he succeeded, he would be able to help the rest of the group reach stardom as well.

In 1999 Nelly secured a solo recording contract with Fo'Reel Entertainment/Universal Records. "When I met Nelly, his whole charisma and style [were] just different," recalled Fo'Reel executive Cudda Love. "Like when you heard [the rap artist Notorious] B.I.G. for the first time, he didn't sound like anybody. 2Pac didn't sound like anybody. Snoop Dogg didn't sound like anybody. It was the same way with Nelly."

Country Grammar

After signing with Universal, Nelly called on the St. Lunatics to join him in the recording studio. Backed by his old friends, Nelly released his first solo effort on the Universal label in 2000. Called *Country Grammar* — a reference to the local dialect spoken by black communities in St. Louis — the

Nelly's Country Grammar *made the rap artist a nationally recognized star.*

album caused an immediate sensation in the music world. It quickly rose to number one on the *Billboard* album charts and stayed there for several weeks. The single most popular track on the CD was the title song, "Country Grammar," which showcased Nelly's ability to combine singing with rapping. It also highlighted the singer's ability to build a song out of simple elements. For example, the tune's refrain — "down, down baby" — was taken from a children's game that Nelly and his friends had played while growing up. The single ultimately reached the top of the *Billboard* rap singles chart and stayed there longer than any other rap song released that year.

The runaway success of *Country Grammar* put St. Louis on the hip-hop map. Reviewers noted that the songs on *Country Grammar* had a different style than those performed by popular East and West coast rappers. Nelly's songs did explore many of the same themes as rap songs from the coasts, such as sex, crime, violence, and expensive cars. But the influence of St. Louis, where the blues and jazz are very popular, could be clearly heard throughout Nelly's work. Many music critics loved Nelly's approach. *Time,* for example, praised the album for "what many other current hip-hop releases lack: strong, sure hooks. The rhythms are vigorous, the production is crisp, and Nelly's rapping manages to be both laid back and engaging." Several songs on the album, including "Batter Up" and "Steal the Show," featured the St. Lunatics, and it was clear that Nelly had no intention of leaving the group behind. "The biggest surprise on *Country Grammar,*" said the *Washington Post,* "is Nelly's crew. The St. Lunatics appear on most of the album and . . . each member seems to be a credible talent in his own right."

—— **"** ——

"When I met Nelly, his whole charisma and style [were] just different," said one record executive. "Like when you heard [the rap artist Notorious] B.I.G. for the first time, he didn't sound like anybody. 2Pac didn't sound like anybody. Snoop Dogg didn't sound like anybody. It was the same way with Nelly."

—— **"** ——

Country Grammar sold 10 million copies in the two years following its release, surpassing the sales of such established stars as Eminem, Britney Spears, and 'N Sync. Nelly also raked in an array of honors for the recording, including a 2000 World Music Award (as Best-Selling New Artist) and two Grammy nominations. He was even invited to perform at the 2001 Super Bowl. But as Nelly's fame and fortune grew, he also drew criticism from some people for his lyrics and subject matter. Many listeners were offended by his swearing and his album's focus on sex and partying. St. Louis Mayor Clarence Harmon even refused to issue a proclamation honoring the local rap artist in 2000 because one of his song titles contained a four-letter word.

Less than six months after the release of *Country Grammar,* Nelly starred in *Snipes,* an independent movie set in the world of hip-hop. He plays the role of a rap star named Prolifik who is kidnapped by gang members the night before his highly anticipated first album is scheduled for release. After the film's release, director Richard Murray gave high marks to Nelly for his professionalism. "I know how musicians and recording artists approach acting," he said. "They take it as a joke. No such case with Nelly. He really approached it from a standpoint of someone taking the challenge as an actor." Unfortunately, the film did not attract large numbers of moviegoers, and it received mostly harsh reviews. A critic writing for the *Indianapolis Recorder*, for example, claimed that the film "reduces the African-American inner-city experience to a glorified ghetto . . . where guns, knives, expletives, and racial epithets lead and reason lags far behind."

Back to the Recording Studio

Nelly used his success with *Country Grammar* to help the St. Lunatics land a record deal of their own with Universal. He also performed with them on the resulting CD, which was released in 2001. Unfortunately, one of the group's members was not around to share in the achievement: Lavell Webb—known as "City Spud" to the St. Lunatics—had been sent to prison in November 1999 for his involvement in an armed robbery. The group named their album *Free City* in his honor, and Nelly started wearing a Band-Aid on his left cheek as a "symbol of solidarity" with City Spud.

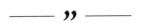

"I don't sound like anyone [else], I've got a style that's all my own," declared Nelly. *"I like to think of my music as a jazz form of hip-hop."*

Bristling with head-bobbing rhythms and lyrics celebrating a hard-partying lifestyle, the songs on *Free City* immediately caused a buzz in the music world. The album debuted at No. 3 on the Billboard 200 album charts, and it eventually sold more than one million copies. *Free City* also confirmed the St. Lunatics' pride in their St. Louis roots. The band members even chose the song "Midwest Swing," which describes their hometown in positive terms, as the album's lead single.

Indeed, while some other popular singers and bands have tried to downplay their local origins so that their music will appeal to the widest possible audience, Nelly has never tried to deny his Midwestern background. Nelly's brand of rap "has a relaxed feel that gives the rhythms and the rhymes their distinctive flavor," the London *Independent* observed. But Nelly himself prefers the word "swing"—the jazzy form of hip-hop characteristic of St. Louis—to describe his more "soulful" style of rap. "Swing is a Midwest thing," Nelly explained to one interviewer. "It's in our walk, the way we dance, our swagger."

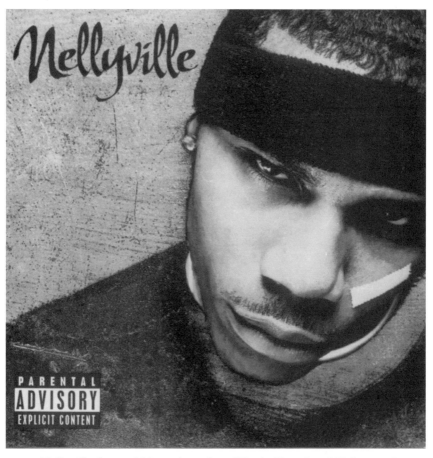

Nellyville *featured hit tracks such as "Hot in Herre" and "Dilemma."*

Nellyville

Shortly after the release of Free City, Nelly and the St. Lunatics joined the 2001 MTV Total Request Live Tour. Nelly then returned to the recording studio, where he put together his second solo album for Universal. The final product, called *Nellyville*, was released in 2002. As with his earlier recordings, Nelly paid tribute to his hometown in a song. The title track describes an idealized version of the crime-ridden neighborhood in which he grew up. "Imagine blocks and blocks of no cocaine with no gunplay/ ain't nobody shot, so ain't no news that day," Nelly sings, adding that in his dream world, everyone has "40 acres and a pool/6 bedrooms, 4 baths with a jacuzz/6-car garage, full paved and smooth/Full front and back deck/Enough room to land a jet."

Another *Nellyville* song, called "#1," describes what it's like to be a hip-hop star. The tune was selected for the soundtrack of the movie *Training Day,* starring Denzel Washington. But it also triggered angry words from hip-hop artist KRS-One. He felt that Nelly's song was full of empty boasts and claimed that one of the song's lines — "Boat sank and it ain't left the dock, mad /cause I'm hot, he just mad 'cause he's not" — was aimed directly at him. KRS-One also accused Nelly of "selling out" because he invited white pop artists like 'N Sync's Justin Timberlake to make guest appearances on the album.

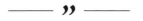

> "I think that nowadays people are turning to music for the positive side," said Nelly. "With all the stuff that been going on in the world, I think people are starting to realize that, yo, maybe we do need to chill out a little more."

Critical reaction to *Nellyville* was mixed as well. *Rolling Stone* claimed that Nelly had "one of the catchiest rhyme flows to ever hit the pop charts" and praised him for being "clear-eyed about his success, his art, who he is and where he's headed." But the magazine accused him of "going through the motions" on some of his songs. *Time,* meanwhile, called Nelly's rhymes "emptier than the St. Louis arch," but admitted that he "raps in a Southern-inflected sing-song so bouncy and joy-filled that he could read the Cardinals' box scores and the world would bob its collective head." For his part, Nelly strongly defends his emphasis on partying and fun times in his lyrics. "I think that nowadays people are turning to music for the positive side," he said. "With all the stuff that been going on in the world, I think people are starting to realize that, yo, maybe we do need to chill out a little more."

In any event, negative comments from critics did not seem to have any effect on the album's sales. *Nellyville* sold two million copies within a month of its release, and it eventually netted Nelly two Grammy Awards and six Billboard Music Awards. Two of the tracks on *Nellyville* proved particularly popular. "Hot in Herre" (pronounced "hurr" in imitation of the way people from St. Louis draw out their *r*'s) describes a party in which everyone is so hot they start taking their clothes off. "Dilemma," which featured singer Kelly Rowland from Destiny's Child, tells the story of a young woman with a baby who isn't happy with the baby's father but can't seem to turn her back on him. "Dilemma" climbed to the top spot on the Billboard charts

Nelly performs with Kelly Rowland at the 2003 Grammy Awards.

and stayed there for 10 weeks, the longest period in which any rap song had claimed the No. 1 spot. When asked to explain the popularity of these and other songs, Nelly simply declared that "I don't sound like anyone [else]. I've got a style that's all my own. . . . I like to think of my music as a jazz form of hip-hop."

Reaching Out to Kids

During his recording career, Nelly has paid tribute to his St. Louis roots in several songs. But he has also devoted time and money to improving the lives of the children growing up in the city's poorest neighborhoods. After the release of his first album, he started visiting inner city high schools to try to convince kids not to drop out. And after *Nellyville* rocketed to the top of the charts, he promised to make appearances at St. Louis schools on days when state-required standardized tests were being given. He and the St. Lunatics subsequently popped up to play basketball and talk to stu-

*Nelly and fellow rapper P. Diddy (left) perform during a 2003
appearance on the "Tonight Show."*

dents at a number of schools in inner-city St. Louis. School administrators
later claimed that Nelly's efforts gave a tremendous boost to school atten-
dance.

In 2002 Missouri Governor Bob Holden issued a proclamation praising
Nelly and the St. Lunatics for their involvement in the schools. Some people criticized the proclamation, given the rough language and heavy sexual
content of their songs. But the governor's office defended the decision.
"The governor is not saying he agrees with the lyrics' content," said a
spokesperson. "But what he does agree with is . . . that these young men
used their success to improve the quality of education in St. Louis."

HOME AND FAMILY

Nelly has one daughter, Chanel, and one son, Cornell III (who is called
Tre). He and the children's mother were together for several years, but he
does not like to comment publicly on the current status of their relationship. "Right now, we each do our thing, and take care of the kids the way
it's supposed to be."

When he is not touring, Nelly lives in St. Louis, where he currently owns two houses. "I'm just more of a Midwest guy," he likes to say. He bought one of the houses for his mother, Rhonda Mack, who retired in 2000 after 30 years in the fast food business. Today, Mack, who describes herself as her son's biggest fan, helps manage Nelly's charitable activities.

MAJOR INFLUENCES

One of Nelly's first childhood heroes was Ozzie Smith, a defensive shortstop for the St. Louis Cardinals baseball team in the 1980s and 1990s. "I wanted to be him. He had fundamentals and flash," he says. "Ozzie was the best shortstop ever. I used to do back flips when I played shortstop because he did it. I wanted to be Number One because that's the number he wore."

Nelly also admires pop star Michael Jackson. "He was the king, regardless of what he's doing or how he looks today. He's like history — he captured the whole world. He paved the way for a lot of [us]."

HOBBIES AND OTHER INTERESTS

Nelly still loves to play baseball, although he does not play as often as he would like. "I don't get much free time," Nelly admits, "so when I have some I really just like to chill out. It depends on where I am. If I'm at home in St. Louis, I'll go to the community center and play with the same Little League guys I've been playing with since I was 12."

"I don't get much free time," Nelly admits, "so when I have some I really just like to chill out.... If I'm at home in St. Louis, I'll go to the community center and play with the same Little League guys I've been playing with since I was 12."

Nelly has used the proceeds from his albums to establish a foundation called 4Sho4Kids. This charitable organization seeks to improve the quality of life for children with developmental disabilities, especially those born with Down Syndrome or drug addictions. "A large portion of my audience is kids and if I can help them as well as they've supported me, it's beautiful for both sides," Nelly declared. In addition, the rap star has expressed interest in starting a nationwide donor drive on behalf of patients in need of bone marrow transplants. With this purpose in mind, Nelly's foundation has announced a "Jes Us 4 Jackie" campaign. The campaign is named for his sister Jackie Donahue, who suffers from leukemia and needs a bone marrow transplant to help her fight off the disease.

Nelly's commercial ventures include a line of urban streetwear for young men between the ages of 13 and 30 called Vokal (Very Organized Kids Always Learning). To promote Vokal, he recently became one of the first African-Americans to become part-owner of a NASCAR racing team. He hopes to hire a minority driver for the team some day. In addition, Nelly has started a production/management company to represent up-and-coming rap and hip-hop artists from the St. Louis area.

RECORDINGS

Country Grammar, 2000
Free City, 2001 (with the St. Lunatics)
Nellyville, 2002

HONORS AND AWARDS

Source Award: 2000 (two awards), Best New Artist of the Year and Best Album of the Year, for *Country Grammar*
BET Award (Black Entertainment Television): 2001, Best New Artist
MTV Video Music Award: 2001, Best Rap Video, for "Ride Wit Me"
Soul Train Music Award: 2001, Best R&B/Soul or Rap New Artist, for "Country Grammar"; 2003, for Entertainer of the Year
American Music Award: 2002, Favorite Rap/Hip-Hop Artist
Grammy Award: 2003 (two awards), Best Male Rap Solo Performance, for "Hot in Herre," and Best Rap/Sung Collaboration (with Kelly Rowland) for "Dilemma"
American Music Award: 2003, Fan Choice Artist

FURTHER READING

Books

Contemporary Black Biography, 2002

Periodicals

Current Biography Yearbook, 2002
Daily Telegraph (London), Nov. 2, 2000, p.25
Ebony, Sep. 2002, p.142
Entertainment Weekly, Aug. 2, 2002, p.38
Indianapolis Recorder, Sep. 6, 2002, p.3

Interview, Sep. 2002, p.88
Jet, July 30, 2001, p.32
Los Angeles Times, July 21, 2002, p.F4
New York Times, June 23, 2002, p.L1
Newsweek, Nov. 11, 2002, p.71
Rolling Stone, Nov. 9, 2000, p.55; Sep. 14, 2000, p.64
Seventeen, Mar. 2003, p.147
USA Today, Sep. 29, 2000, p.E5; Sep. 3, 2002, p.D1
YM, Apr. 2003, p.6

Online Databases

Biography Resource Center Online, 2003, article from *Contemporary Black Biography,* 2002

ADDRESS

Nelly
Uptown/Universal Records
1755 Broadway
New York, NY 10019

WORLD WIDE WEB SITES

http:// www.nelly.net

Gwen Stefani 1969-
American Singer and Songwriter
Lead Singer for the Rock Band No Doubt

BIRTH

Gwen Renee Stefani was born on October 3, 1969, in Fullerton, California. Her father, Dennis, is a marketing consultant. Her mother, Patricia, is a full-time homemaker. Both of her parents are devout Catholics of Italian descent. Stefani is one of four children. Her older brother Eric founded the band No Doubt in 1987 and later worked as an animator on the TV show "The Simpsons." She also has a younger sister, Jill, and a younger brother.

YOUTH

Stefani grew up in Anaheim, California, 30 miles south of downtown Los Angeles. The family's home was so close to Disneyland that ashes from the Disney fireworks displays sometimes floated into their front yard. Looking back on her childhood, Stefani claimed that she was an ordinary, suburban girl from a "goody-two-shoes" but warm and loving family. She also indicated that she was "chubby" throughout her youth, a condition that eventually prompted her to compete on her high school's swim team. "I joined the swim team because I wanted to get skinny," she said. "I grew up ten pounds overweight and never had a date."

Stefani was exposed to music at an early age. Her parents played folk music themselves, and they enjoyed listening to many different styles of music in their home. As a child, Stefani particularly liked soundtracks from such musicals as *Evita, Annie,* and *The Muppet Movie.* She especially loved the 1960s movie musical *The Sound of Music.* "The whole soundtrack is really special to my heart," she said.

"I was rebellious in the sense that I wasn't into popular music," Stefani stated. "It was like, 'I'm into ska, nobody knows what it is. I'm cool, you're not.' I wasn't a cheerleader, never had a lot of girlfriends — just one best girlfriend."

Stefani's older brother Eric also loved music. "Growing up, my brother was the one with all the talent and all the focus," she recalled. "I had him, so I didn't have to do anything, you know?" She even credits Eric with introducing her to ska music, a form of dance music similar to reggae. "[Eric was] a really quirky, creative guy who discovered ska music, and we all became attracted to the hyperactivity and energy," she explained. "My brother was sort of the leader of the family so the rest of us became obsessed with it."

By Stefani's teen years, ska music had achieved cult favorite status in Southern California. But she credits one particular ska band, called Madness, for her enduring affection for the musical genre. In 1983, when Stefani was about 14, she was thrilled to hear that Madness was opening for English rock star David Bowie at a nearby concert hall. "My brother got to go, but my dad said I was too young. I cried myself to sleep on the couch because Madness is my favorite band of all time," Stefani remembered. "The next thing I know, my mom put the phone on my ear, and it was my dad saying, 'Are you too tired to go to the concert? I got tickets.' I was mesmerized by Madness."

As a teen, Stefani even saw her love for ska music as a way of establishing a unique identity. "I was rebellious in the sense that I wasn't into popular music," she said. "It was like, 'I'm into ska, nobody knows what it is. I'm cool; you're not.' I wasn't a cheerleader, never had a lot of girlfriends—just one best girlfriend."

The other major area in which Stefani proclaimed her individuality was in the clothes she wore. "Ever since puberty, it has been all about doing something that was a little bit different from everyone else, while at the same time showing off my favorite features and hiding the ones I'm not a fan of," Stefani explained. During high school she combed through thrift stores or sewed her own clothes to get the look she wanted. Sometimes, her mother's skills as a seamstress came in handy as well. For example, her mother helped her make a high school prom dress that was a replica of the one Grace Kelly wore in the Alfred Hitchcock film, *Rear Window*. "I've always been obsessed with the days of the Hollywood starlet," Stefani declared.

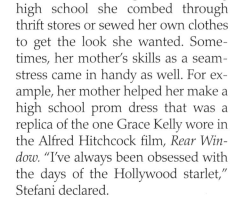

"When I look back at some of the horrible things people did to others in high school, it breaks my heart," Stefani said. "When you judge people and say things that may hurt someone else, it may go deeper than you think. So try to be as open-minded as you can. At this age, you're still trying to find yourself."

EDUCATION

Stefani grew up with a form of dyslexia, a type of learning disability that causes readers to confuse the order of letters in words. As a result, she struggled in many of her classes. "I had a really hard time learning in school," she admitted. For many years, she did not even know that she was suffering from a dyslexic condition. "I didn't know that and it was really challenging for me," she said. "I had horrible fights with my mom because I was frustrated that I couldn't learn."

Stefani also has mixed memories of high school's social scene. Her love for music blossomed during this period of her life, but she witnessed numerous instances when students were cruel to one another. "When I look back at some of the horrible things people did to others in high school, it breaks my heart," she said. "Think about the fact that you don't know everything about another person. You don't know where they are coming from. You don't know the circumstances in their family. For instance, one of my best friends and bandmates shot himself at age 18. We didn't even know the pain he was going through. . . . When you judge people and say things that may hurt someone else, it may go deeper than you think. So try to be as open-minded as you can. At this age, you're still trying to find yourself."

Despite her reading difficulties, Stefani graduated from Loara High School in Anaheim. She also attended Fullerton Junior College and California State University at Fullerton. "I wanted to be educated. I wanted to be a strong member of society and know what I was talking about," she said. "When I went to college, I said that I'm just going to try my hardest. Going to college saved me."

CAREER HIGHLIGHTS

Joining the Band

Stefani's brother Eric and a classmate named John Spence founded No Doubt as a ska band in December 1986. Named after Spence's habit of saying "no doubt" all the time, the band soon came to include Stefani. She initially shared lead and backing vocals with Spence, a high-energy performer known for his punk-style screaming and back-flips on stage. In December 1987, however, Spence shocked and saddened his bandmates by committing suicide. "He was a very important part of the band," Stefani said. "It still haunts us in a way. When your friend dies like that, and it's so unexpected, it's very traumatic. I think it taught us all a big lesson in how much one person can influence so many different people."

Less than two weeks after Spence died, the band kept an engagement in West Hollywood. During the show, a friend announced from the stage that it would be the band's last appearance. A short time later, though, the band members decided Spence would have wanted them to continue. His death turned out to be only the first of many hurdles that No Doubt would overcome over the years.

After Spence's suicide, Stefani was reluctant to take on the role of lead singer. For a year or so she shared the spotlight with bandmate Alan Meade. But when Meade left the band, Stefani nervously took center stage. "It took a lot of convincing to get her to the lead-singer position," recalled one former band member.

At first, Stefani worried that she was not aggressive enough to satisfy the band's high-energy fans. But she compensated by displaying a flair for sexy showmanship. Stefani soon perfected a highly energetic and theatrical style on stage, with a purring and growling sound that became a band signature. She also developed a striking appearance, sporting bleached plat-

No Doubt released its self-titled debut album in 1992.
Band members included (from right) Gwen Stefani, Tony Kanal,
Tom Dumont, Adrian Young, and Eric Stefani.

inum blond hair, dramatic make-up, and outrageous outfits that combined masculine and feminine qualities. For example, she often roamed the stage in baggy combat trousers and a push-up bra, wearing candy-apple-red lipstick and clunky Doc Martens shoes. She loved to bare her midriff, and her bare bellybutton became a trademark.

Stefani also credited No Doubt's surging popularity among California music fans to the band's mix of musical styles. Indeed, various band members brought different musical styles to No Doubt's mix, from funk and heavy metal to punk and classic rock. Stefani and her brother Eric, meanwhile, made sure that the band never strayed too far from its ska and reggae roots. "I always thought we could never be cool enough or tough enough or hard enough, because of me being a girl," she recalled. "But we could always mix it up a lot more—I love to sing all sorts of stuff, ballads and punk songs. Our show is so physical. The music is raw, broken down to the bare bones."

Yet despite their growing popularity, Stefani claimed that she and the other band members—brother Eric, bass player Tony Kanal, guitarist Tom Dumont, and drummer Adrian Young—never dared dream of major or long-term success. "We were doing it because we were passionate and couldn't help ourselves," she said. "We all went to school and went to college and we all had back-up plans. No one was ever intending for this to be our careers."

Reaching for Stardom

In 1992, No Doubt's popularity in southern California convinced the Interscope label to sign them to a record contract. Later that year, the band released their first album, *No Doubt*. Eric Stefani, who remained the artistic heart of the group, wrote most of the music and guided the production of the debut album. The release blended serious relationship songs with lighthearted pieces about "pigging out" and Eric's wisdom-tooth extraction, all set to a bouncy, fun beat. Unfortunately for the band, the recording was mostly ignored because it was so different from "grunge rock," the dominant musical style of the early 1990s. The group toured to support the record—an experience Eric Stefani clearly did not enjoy—but it remained a commercial disappointment.

———— **"** ————

"I always thought we could never be cool enough or tough enough or hard enough, because of me being a girl," Stefani admitted. "But we could always mix it up a lot more—I love to sing all sorts of stuff, ballads and punk songs."

———— **"** ————

The album's poor performance concerned Interscope. When the band presented new material for a second album, Interscope repeatedly asking Stefani and her bandmates to go back and start over. The label's attitude angered the band, and in 1995 No Doubt took matters into their own hands. They distributed their second record, *The Beacon Street Collection*, as an independent release. The band liked the songs on *Beacon Street*, but it did not attract much attention from the public. Music critics gave it a mixed reception, too. At this point, Stefani and the other members of the band began to feel the stress of an uncertain future.

Around this time, however, the band caught the attention of a small record label called Trauma. The label's chief loved No Doubt's music and wanted to bring out their next record. That suited Interscope, which continued to serve as the band's distributor. The deal came as a great relief to the group, but it failed to soothe Eric Stefani, who was fed up with the hassles and uncertainties of the music business. By this time, he had even stopped coming to band practice sessions — even though they took place in his own house. It came as no surprise, then, when he announced his decision to leave the group to focus on a career as an animator.

Eric's departure forced the other band members to fill the creative and musical void he left behind. To her surprise, Stefani discovered she had more room to develop as a songwriter. "In the early days, my brother wrote most of the music and I was the one sitting on the couch watching *The Brady Bunch*," Stefani said. After he left the band, however, she wrote many of the lyrics and music for No Doubt's third album, *Tragic Kingdom*.

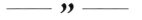

> "I'm a more old-fashioned kind of girl, a real girly-girl," Stefani said. "At the same time, being in a band for eight years with all these guys, you really see the difference between being a girl and a guy."

As it turned out, Stefani had plenty of real-life song-writing material for the record. In the midst of preparing the album, Stefani's eight-year romance with No Doubt bass guitarist Tony Kanal came to an end. She resisted the break-up — "the amputation," she called it — but when it happened, she tapped into her emotions to write several songs. In "Don't Speak," for example, she used lyrics that reflected the feelings of the heartbroken everywhere: "Don't speak/ I know just what you're saying/ So please stop explaining/ Don't tell me 'cause it hurts." In "Happy Now?" on the other hand, Stefani gently taunts a man who has ended a romance but then wants to get back together. And in songs such as "End It on This," Stefani declares her independence from boyfriends. Stefani later described the album as "happy music with bummed-out lyrics."

Tragic Kingdom Breaks Through

When *Tragic Kingdom* was released in late 1995, "we were hanging on a thread," Stefani admitted. "We carried this album for three years and it went through some hard times. By the end, we were back in school, had

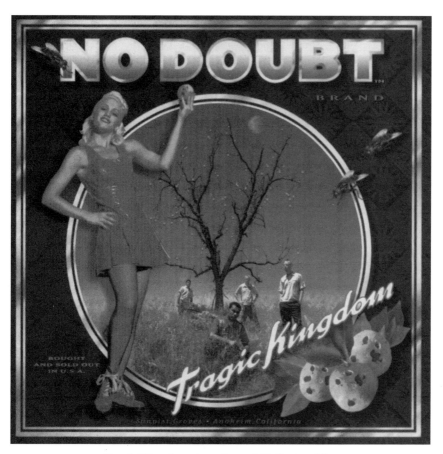

Tragic Kingdom *transformed Stefani and her bandmates into major rock stars.*

jobs, had all our back-up plans in place [in case the album failed]." But instead, *Tragic Kingdom* took the music world by storm. Snapped up by music fans eager for an upbeat alternative to grunge rock, the album soared up the charts. *Tragic Kingdom* became one of the top-selling albums of 1996, and it eventually sold 15 million copies worldwide.

To Stefani's surprise, the album's biggest hit was "Just a Girl," a song she wrote about society's patronizing attitudes toward women. "I'm really not the type of person that's a big feminist. I'm a more old-fashioned kind of girl, a real girly-girl," Stefani said. "At the same time, being in a band for eight years with all these guys, you really see the difference between being a girl and a guy. The song kind of reflects those differences with a sarcastic edge."

Stefani performs at a No Doubt concert in New York City.

After eight years together, the members of No Doubt regarded their "overnight" international success as if it were a happy dream. "That we got on the radio is the weirdest thing in the world," Stefani said. "I'm driving in my car, and the DJ's saying our name, and it's like, 'Hey, everybody, that's us!'" Stefani and her bandmates wore their success lightly, even as they savored every moment. "I really try to enjoy every second and be really aware," Stefani said. "I don't take it for granted when somebody says, 'Can I have your autograph?' I give it with joy."

During No Doubt's 1995 concert tour in support of *Tragic Kingdom,* Stefani emerged as the band's most visible member. Reviewing one concert appearance, *Hollywood Reporter* declared that she "practically radiated soon-to-be-huge stage presence, managing to come off sexy, coy, and ferocious simultaneously," But Stefani's growing stardom created tension with the band's three male members, all of whom felt that they were being ignored. The situation worsened when *Spin* splashed a photo of Stefani — without the other No Doubt members — on its cover. Stefani did what she could to discourage the favoritism, but it did not make her bandmates feel much better.

Meanwhile, Stefani and Kanal faced the difficulty of working together after their break-up. "You break up with your boyfriend that you've been with for almost eight years, and you're writing about him, and he's in your group and he's going to play the song that's about him," she said. "And then you travel with him on a bus 24 hours a day. It's a really weird situation — but we've made it work." She noted that neither of them has tried to hide the fact that many of *Tragic Kingdom* songs were inspired by their relationship. "Later, we started thinking we should be more quiet about it. But how could we know the band was going to get big?"

> *"You break up with your boyfriend that you've been with for almost eight years, and you're writing about him, and he's in your group and he's going to play the song that about him," said Stefani. "And then you travel with him on a bus 24 hours a day. It's a really weird situation — but we've made it work."*

As the tour continued, Stefani met Gavin Rossdale, lead singer of the British rock band Bush. The two singers started a romance, but their busy touring schedules and home bases — hers in California and his in London, England — made it difficult for them to see one another.

Return of Saturn

No Doubt toured for more than two years after the release of *Tragic Kingdom*. The traveling took its toll, however. In the fall of 1996, for example, doctors ordered Stefani to stop singing temporarily after she devel-

Stefani and rap star Eve (right) teamed up to record the hit song "Let Me Blow Ya Mind."

oped nodules on her throat. At the conclusion of the tour, she returned to her parents' home for a rest. But instead, she settled into what she described as "a weird kind of depression. Maybe not a depression so much as just a cloudy, confusing state for a couple of years."

Stefani gradually realized that she was not entirely happy with her life, despite her professional success. She was approaching 30 years of age, but she felt lonely and far away from her long-time dream of having children. "I think everyone gets to a point in their life where they grow up and go, 'Wow, this is me now. I'm not just a kid. This is what I'm doing," she said.

Stefani's bandmates were in a reflective mood, too. "I think we all knew it," said No Doubt guitarist Tom Dumont. "We got together and decided that rather than repeat *Tragic Kingdom*, we should have a goal—to improve as songwriters. To stretch." Stefani took this goal to heart. At Rossdale's suggestion, she began to keep a journal. She also studied the work of writers she admired, including folksinger Joni Mitchell and Sylvia Plath, a gifted American poet who killed herself in the early 1960s.

In 2000 No Doubt released its fourth album, titled *Return of Saturn*. The title refers to the 29 and a half years it takes the planet Saturn to revolve around the sun. Stefani reckons that this is about the same amount of time that most people need to figure out what they want to do with their lives.

Several of the songs on the album displayed the band's interest in exploring issues of personal growth and happiness. On "A Simple Kind of Life," for example, Stefani muses on the crossroads she faces at 30: "I always thought I'd be a mom/Sometimes I wish for a mistake/The longer I wait the more selfish I get." Stefani said that many people believe this song simply expresses her longing to get married and have babies. But she claimed that it is "more about how I used to think that's all I ever wanted and the confusion of realizing that I am more faithful to my freedom than I ever thought I could be. And that's scary." The song "Bathwater" rollicks like an old show song, but expresses more unfulfilled longing: "I still love to wash in your old bathwater/ Love to think that you couldn't love another." Stefani acknowledged that her boyfriend Rossdale inspired these songs, along with the not-so-subtle "Marry Me."

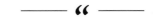

"We feel so good about [Return of Saturn]," said Stefani. "We're all kind of shocked at the chemistry we had together, and the amount of growth from **Tragic Kingdom** *to this record. It's a huge step for us, not a little baby one."*

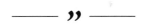

All of the members of No Doubt expressed deep satisfaction with *Return of Saturn*. "We feel so good about it," confirmed Stefani. "We're all kind of shocked at the chemistry we had together, and the amount of growth from *Tragic Kingdom* to this record. It's a huge step for us, not a little baby one." But critics did not completely agree. *Time* praised the record and declared that Stefani performed her "bittersweet" songs very well. But *Entertainment Weekly* accused Stefani of having "regressed emotionally," claiming that Stefani's lyrics "incessantly circle around the same theme: terminal insecurity." *Rolling Stone*, meanwhile, praised it as a "subtle and heartfelt" album, but charged that some portions of it were "a little overcooked." Music fans also gave *Return of Saturn* a mixed reception. After debuting at No. 2 on the

Billboard chart of top-selling records, it slid down the chart fairly quickly. It eventually sold 1.4 million copies in the United States, a healthy total but far less than the sales reaped by *Tragic Kingdom.*

In 2001 Stefani stayed in the music spotlight with guest appearances on two songs recorded by other major musical stars. The first of these was "South Side," composed by electronica musician Moby. For the second, she teamed up with Philadelphia rapper Eve to record "Let Me Blow Ya Mind." Initially, Stefani was unsure about recording a song with Eve. "It was like, 'Should I be doing another side thing? Ya know, Are people gonna think that I'm just like the side sausage?" she recalled. But she desperately wanted to work with Eve's producer, hip-hop legend Dr. Dre. Stefani later admitted that the recording sessions for "Let Me Blow Ya Mind" wore her down. "I probably sang the chorus for like two-and-a half hours straight," she said. "[Dr. Dre] beat me up as a singer. He really challenged me. He had one thing in his head, and I wasn't hearing the same thing in my head." Ultimately, however, they recorded a song that everyone liked.

> **"*[We] were having dance parties every night, inviting people back and listening to a lot of Jamaican dancehall — just having the most fun,*" said band member Tony Kanal. "*So, when we started making* [Rock Steady], *we decided to put everything else aside and just have a great time. The thinking was, 'While we're writing music, let's keep the fun going.'*"**

A few months later, Stefani and Eve received a 2002 Grammy Award for Best Rap Song Collaboration for "Let Me Blow Ya Mind." In addition, her work with Moby and Eve brought her to the attention of legions of electronica and hip-hop fans. "Even the big, beefy security guards now recognize me: 'Hey, Gwen, wazzzz up? You're dope, man.' I love that!" she said. "And all I did was sing on that song!"

Rock Steady

In 2001 No Doubt returned to the upbeat sound of their early days for *Rock Steady,* their fifth album. Bathed in good spirits and high times, it blended Jamaican dancehall (a form of slowed-down reggae), new wave, and hip-hop music into a crowd-pleasing series of songs. The recording also featured a wide array of guest stars from the worlds of ska, reggae, and funk.

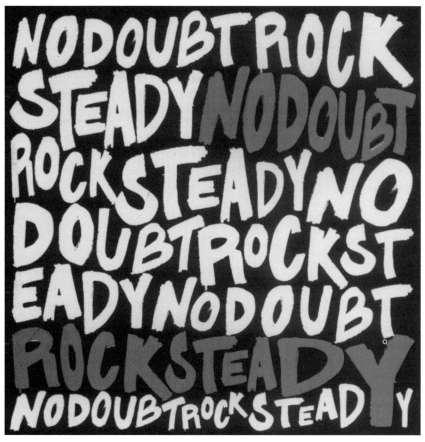

Rock Steady *was praised by critics as one of No Doubt's strongest releases.*

Kanal later said that the spirit of *Rock Steady* could be traced back to the band's *Return of Saturn* tour. "[We] were having dance parties every night, inviting people back and listening to a lot of Jamaican dancehall—just having the most fun," he said. "So, when we started making this record, we decided to put everything else aside and just have a great time. The thinking was, "While we're writing music, let's keep the fun going." With this perspective in mind, the band refused to spend months agonizing over every song. "We're not taking ourselves so seriously," Stefani said. "It's like, get over it. We're in a . . . band and we're really lucky to be doing what we do."

Reviewers loved the results. "As comebacks go, [*Rock Steady* is] up there with Elvis," pronounced the English music magazine *NME*. *Entertainment Weekly*—which had slammed *Saturn Returns*—heaped praise on the band as well. "[This] beat-heavy quickie turns out to be the best album they've ever hatched. . . . *Rock Steady* mostly ditches ska, not to mention the overthink of *Return of Saturn,* and replaces it with doses of the leaner, meaner pop No Doubt was born to make." *Newsweek,* meanwhile, called the album No Doubt's "most risky, varied and creative music to date." According to the review, Stefani's voice displayed a " new confidence: she's able to smooth out and flow on balmy, Caribbean-style ballads like 'Underneath It All,' then kick in hard on quirky, slamming dance tunes such as 'Hey, Baby' and 'Making Out'."

In the meantime, Stefani continued to be a fashion trendsetter. Long known for her appearance — an unlikely blending of Hollywood starlet and "riot grrrl" styles — she started to wear clothing by such top designers as Vivienne Westwood and John Galliano. She also has been credited with contributing to the popularity of everything from push-up bras and teeth braces to pink hair and Indian bindis (the stick-on jewel in the center of a woman's forehead). Stefani admitted that her influence on fashion continues to astonish her. "I was the type who thought I could never influence anyone, this loser from Anaheim," she said. "I think I've been able to fool a lot of people. Because I know I'm a dork, I'm a geek."

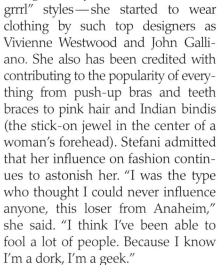

> **Stefani has admitted that her influence on fashion continues to astonish her. "I was the type who thought I could never influence anyone," said Stefani. "I think I've been able to fool a lot of people. Because I know I'm a dork, I'm a geek."**

The success of *Rock Steady* enabled No Doubt to claim a number of desirable touring slots. They shared the stage with the famous Irish rock band U2 on a number of dates, and even opened for the Rolling Stones. The album also earned the band its first ever Grammy Award, when "Hey, Baby" won the 2003 Grammy for Best Pop Performance by a Group.

Since the tour supporting *Rock Steady,* No Doubt has been on a break. Stefani has kept busy, however. In early 2003 she announced that she was preparing a line of leather goods, from CD cases to handbags, for a major manufacturer. She also has announced plans to launch her own ready-to-wear fashion line, called Lamb. Finally, Stefani is expected to make her acting debut in a film biography of the famous American millionaire Howard Hughes. The movie will be directed by Martin Scorcese, one of America's most respected filmmakers, and stars Leonardo DiCaprio in the role of

Hughes, along with an all-star cast. Stefani is slated to portray glamorous actress Jean Harlow.

MARRIAGE AND FAMILY

Stefani married her longtime boyfriend, Gavin Rossdale of the British grunge-rock band Bush, in September 2002. "It was fairly obvious that this was going to happen," stated Rossdale's father. "They are a good couple." Stefani has stated that she wants to start a family. "I feel very romantic about the idea because I think Gavin's going to be the most incredible dad," she said. "I'm excited about seeing him as a husband first. But if I got pregnant tomorrow, I'd be like, 'Yeeahhh'!"

Stefania and Bush lead singer Gavin Rossdale were married in September 2002.

HOBBIES AND INTERESTS

In addition to fashion and music, Stefani is interested in painting. "I always had this big fantasy that when I get pregnant I'm going to have this little mask on and sit and paint every day and get really fat and have a show at the end with all the paintings," she said. "'The Mind of a Pregnant Woman' would be the name of it."

SELECTED RECORDINGS

No Doubt, 1992
The Beacon Street Collection, 1995
Tragic Kingdom, 1995
Return of Saturn, 2000
Rock Steady, 2001

HONORS AND AWARDS

MTV Music Award: 1997, Best Group Video for "Don't Speak" (with No Doubt)

VH1/Vogue Fashion Awards: 1999, for Most Stylish Video for "New";
    2000, for Most Stylish Video for "Ex-Girlfriend"; 2001, for Most
    Fabionable Female Artist
Grammy Awards: 2002, for Best-Rap Song Collaboration for "Let Me Blow
    Ya Mind" (with Eve); 2003, for Best Pop Performance by a Duo or Group,
    for "Hey, Baby" (with No Doubt)

FURTHER READING

Books

Contemporary Musicians, Vol. 20, 1997

Periodicals

Billboard, Nov. 24, 2001, p.1
Entertainment Weekly, May 12, 2000, p.32
Los Angeles Times, April 13, 2000, p. F6; Mar. 16, 1996, p. F1; Apr. 2, 1992,
    p. F1
Newsweek, Dec. 17, 2001, p 67
People Weekly, May, 19, 1997, p.105
Rolling Stone, Nov. 8, 2001, p.27; Jul. 6, 2000, p.68; May 1, 1997, p.36
Scholastic Scope, Mar. 11, 2002, p.16
Teen People, Aug. 1, 2002, p.138
Vogue, Oct., 2002, p.354
Washington Post, June 15, 1997, p.G1

Online Databases

Contemporary Musicians, 1997, reproduced in *Biography Resource Center,* 2003

ADDRESS

Gwen Stefani
Interscope Records
2220 Colorado Ave.
Santa Monica, CA 90404

WORLD WIDE WEB SITE

http://www.nodoubt.com

Meg Whitman 1956-

American Business Leader
President and Chief Executive Officer of the eBay
Internet Auction Site

BIRTH

Margaret C. (Meg) Whitman was born on August 4, 1956, in
Cold Spring Harbor, New York. Her affluent hometown is located on Long Island, outside of New York City. Her father,
Hendricks, was a "factor"—a person who lends money to
businesses using their accounts receivable (the funds that their
customers owe to them) to secure the loans. Her mother,

———— " ————

"When I was growing up on Long Island in the '60s and '70s, my parents raised me largely to become a wife and a mother," Whitman recalled. "A career, they said, was something a woman needed only as a backup. You could get a nursing degree or a teaching certificate or learn secretarial skills because those were jobs you could fall back on if something bad happened, like if your husband left you or was hit by a truck. It wasn't that long ago, but it was a very different time and place."

———— " ————

Margaret, was a homemaker who later led delegations and tour groups to China. Meg is the youngest of three children.

YOUTH

Whitman's parents both came from well-established East Coast families. They held conservative political views and social values. In fact, Whitman described her mother as a "rock-ribbed Republican who could wear a Peck & Peck suit," referring to the up-scale department store.

But Whitman credits her mother with teaching her to be adventurous and adaptable. The summer Whitman was six years old, for example, her mother and a friend packed their eight children into a camper for a three-month tour of the United States. When the children got restless and started to squabble, Whitman's mother let them out of the camper to run ahead on the mostly deserted roads. She would trail behind them until they were tired out, then she would pick them up again. Well-meaning truckers occasionally stopped to see if the group needed help. "You could always hear the hiss of the air brakes," Whitman remembered. "We finally put a sign on the back of the camper that said, 'We're OK.'"

Although Whitman's parents taught her to be self-sufficient, they did not always encourage her to pursue a career. "When I was growing up on Long Island in the '60s and '70s, my parents raised me largely to become a wife and mother," Whitman noted. "A career, they said, was something a woman needed only as a backup. You could get a nursing degree or a teaching certificate or learn secretarial skills because those were jobs you could fall back on if something bad happened, like if your husband left you or was hit by a truck. It wasn't that long ago, but it was a very different time and place."

In 1973, when Whitman was a senior in high school, her mother had a life-changing experience that reversed her former attitude about women pursuing careers. She joined a delegation to China organized by Shirley MacLaine, a well-known actress. China had been closed to most outsiders since it adopted a Communist form of government in 1949. (Under a Communist political system, the central government exercises a great deal of control over the lives of citizens. Communism eliminates most private property and gives it to the government to distribute as it sees fit. Communism also places severe restrictions on individual rights and allows the government to control the educations, careers, and cultural experiences of the people.)

MacLaine's delegation to China included several filmmakers who documented the trip. The American visitors learned that Chinese women had much the same level of responsibility as men, whether in factories, farms, or politics. "When Mom came back, she had a whole new point of view on what women could do," Whitman recalled. "She more or less said, 'All that advice I gave you before? Ignore it. You can do anything you want to do. Find a career that you love and that makes you happy, and do that in addition to being a wife and mom.' Here was the most important woman in my life saying basically to just forget what she'd been telling me for the last 15 years."

Her mother's new message really hit home when the delegation's female camera crew came to the Whitman home for dinner. All of the women were accomplished professionals. One was a top documentary filmmaker, and another was the first female technician in her labor union. "From talking to these women, I figured out that the most important thing was to put your head down and do a great job," Whitman said.

Whitman's mother, meanwhile, went on to make a career of leading dele-

—— **"** ——

"When Mom came back [from China], she had a whole new point of view on what women could do," said Whitman. "She more or less said, 'All that advice I gave you before? Ignore it. You can do anything you want to do. Find a career that you love and that makes you happy, and do that in addition to being a wife and mom.' Here was the most important woman in my life saying basically to just forget what she'd been telling me for the last 15 years."

—— ——

gations and tour groups to China. In 2002, at age 82, she returned to China with her daughter to mark an eBay business deal. "It was a poignant moment and, in some ways, like coming full circle, for her to see eBay in China," Whitman wrote. "It was just what she taught me: The possibilities were wide open."

EDUCATION

Whitman attended Princeton University, a top American college located in New Jersey. She originally planned to become a doctor, but the pre-med courses turned her off. "I didn't enjoy it," she stated. "Of course, chemistry, calculus, and physics have nothing to do with being a doctor, but if you're 17 years old, you think, 'This is what being a doctor is going to be about.'" She first realized that she enjoyed business when she began to sell advertising for *Business Today*, a magazine published by Princeton undergraduates. She started learning about the business world by ordering the *Wall Street Journal* — the leading U.S. business newspaper — delivered to her dormitory room.

Whitman earned a bachelor's degree in economics in 1977. She continued her education at prestigious Harvard University, earning a master's degree in business administration in 1979. Whitman excelled in her studies at Harvard, but she admitted that she felt intimidated by some of her classmates. In one class, for example, she sat between a manager from Chemical Bank and a 32-year-old Army platoon commander. "It was the first time in my life I worked hard because I was scared [of failing]," Whitman recalled. "Mostly I work hard because I want to achieve, because I love it."

CAREER HIGHLIGHTS

Working Her Way up the Corporate Ladder

Whitman launched her business career at Procter and Gamble, a large U.S. manufacturer of Ivory soap and other consumer products. Working as a brand assistant and brand manager, her responsibilities included finding the best way to sell a particular product. It was during this time that she made what she called one of her biggest mistakes in business. Without conducting customer research, Whitman decided that a new product, Ivory shampoo, should be colored blue so that it would not be mistaken for dishwashing liquid. But customers were shocked, because Ivory soap had always been pure white. Procter & Gamble quickly changed the shampoo's color to white, and Whitman learned the value of market research.

In 1980 Whitman married Griffith R. Harsh IV, a doctor who was training to become a brain surgeon. When her husband entered a medical residency program in California, she went to work for Bain and Company, a consulting firm. One of her first assignments was to help a college food-service company improve its performance. She visited universities and got first-hand feedback from the students and food-service directors. "It was an early introduction in the importance of talking to customers," she said.

During her eight years at Bain, Whitman learned about establishing effective work cultures—work environments that best motivate employees to succeed. She modeled her ideal work culture on her own co-workers, whom she described as "young, smart, aggressive, fun" people who worked toward "a shared vision and values." Whitman used her expertise to help corporate clients determine their focus and develop "vision statements" to help them reach their goals.

"Meg was willing to mix it up with florists all over the world," said one colleague about her days working at FTD. "She would shake their hands and kiss their babies."

In 1989 Whitman joined the Disney Corporation as a senior vice president of marketing in the consumer products division. In three years at Disney, she helped the company launch a book publishing division and acquire *Discover* magazine. She also oversaw Disney's entry into the world of retail

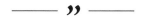

shopping. When she joined the company, there were only three Disney stores in existence. By the time she left, Disney maintained 250 stores, including outlets in Japan.

In 1992 Whitman's husband was named co-director of the brain tumor program at Massachusetts General Hospital. The family subsequently moved to Boston, where Whitman joined Stride Rite Shoes Corporation, a manufacturer of children's shoes, Keds sneakers, and Sperry Topsiders. Whitman rejuvenated the Stride Rite brand and expanded the variety of shoes the company offered. For example, she launched the successful Munchkins line of baby shoes. She also oversaw Stride Rite retail stores and dealers.

During her three years at Stride Rite, Whitman learned that it was critical to involve the entire management team in creating a company strategy. Shortly after joining the company, she wrote down her vision for Stride Rite and passed it out to senior management. "People used to refer to it as

Whitman meets with Pierre Omidyar, founder of eBay.

'Meg's vision,' and that was not a good thing," she said. Whitman later decided to take her team away from the office for a couple of days to develop a vision they could all share in.

In 1995 Whitman accepted a lucrative job offer from Florists' Transworld Delivery (FTD), the flower delivery service. She achieved her dream of leading a major corporation when she was named president and chief executive officer (CEO) shortly after joining FTD. Whitman led the organization's transition from an association owned by florists to a privately owned, for-profit company. Many of the members and managers resisted the plan, but Whitman did her best to convince florists the change was good. "Meg was willing to mix it up with florists all over the world," said a colleague. "She would shake their hands and kiss their babies."

Whitman's reorganization efforts stalled due to infighting among her managers, however. The situation became so frustrating to her that she decided to pursue other career opportunities. In 1997 she left FTD to assume leadership of the Playskool division of Hasbro, one of America's largest toy and game manufacturers. The *New York Times* later described Whitman's FTD experience as one of the biggest disappointments of her career.

Moving to eBay

Whitman remained at Hasbro for only a few months. In November 1997 a corporate recruiter (or "headhunter") asked her to interview for the top job at an Internet start-up company in California. AuctionWeb (as eBay was then called) allowed users to sell goods online to the highest bidder. Whitman told the recruiter that she was not interested. "I had never heard of eBay, and I said, 'I'm not going to move my family 3,000 miles across the country. I'm married to a neurosurgeon, and we have two boys. We aren't going to move our family for this no-name Internet company.' And so I said no, and three weeks later the headhunter called back and said, 'You are perfect for eBay and eBay is perfect for you. I beg you to get on the plane.'" Whitman finally agreed, but only because she thought the recruiter might be able to help her career in the future.

A computer programmer named Pierre Omidyar had launched eBay in September 1995. There's a company legend about how he started the company, although it may or may not be true. Legend says that he originally set up the Internet site to help his girl-friend — a collector of Pez candy dispensers — find a broader network of collectors to trade with. But Omidyar soon found that the appeal of the site went far beyond what he envisioned. It allowed hobbyists and collectors of all sorts of things to share their interests with fellow enthusiasts. The site soon featured Beanie Babies, rare coins, antique glassware, and numerous other items. Sellers posted their items on the site with a description, a minimum bid, and a time period before the sale would be finalized. Buyers then competed for the item until the period of the auction expired. The highest bidder at the deadline claimed the item.

Whitman claims that when she was first asked to head eBay, she said "I'm not going to move my family 3,000 miles across the country. . . . We aren't going to move our family for this no-name Internet company."

At first Omidyar provided his service free of charge. He soon built a foundation of buyers and sellers through word of mouth. Omidyar later introduced a small fee to list an item, as well as a system that automatically charges a small percentage on each item's selling price. The site was so successful that Omidyar quit his day job and incorporated the online venture as a business in May 1996. A year later he sold 22 percent of AuctionWeb to a capital investment firm for $5 million. Around this time, he changed the company name to eBay, in honor of the San Francisco Bay area where it was founded.

During Whitman's initial research into eBay, she was not impressed. "I will never forget, I got on eBay the night before I went to the interview," she recalled. "[The site] was in black and white and there were three components to the site. The first component was the auction business, the second was [Omidyar's] fiancee's web page, and the third was the Ebola virus page, because Pierre was really interested in the Ebola virus [a deadly, highly contagious disease]. And I said, 'I cannot believe I am getting on a plane to go talk about a black-and-white web site called AuctionWeb that has equal billing with the fiancee's web page and the Ebola virus page.' But I had already committed, so I got on the plane."

> "[Taking the job at eBay] was a huge risk," admitted Whitman. "But we loved being in California and we thought that tech would continue to play an increasing role in society, and that being in the heartland of tech for us and our two boys would be positive. And we figured, what's the worst that could happen? I get another job."

The eBay offices in San Jose, California, were a far cry from Whitman's plush corporate world. The rented offices were dingy, and the company's total work force consisted of only 20 employees. But as Whitman learned more about the company's services and history, she recognized that it had enormous potential. The auction site was able to make a large profit because it had so few expenses. All the merchandise came from users, who also made all the arrangements for payment and shipping. Unlike other Internet retailers, eBay did not need to maintain inventory, warehouses, trucks, or a large staff. As a result, eBay grew by leaps and bounds. "This was a tiny company," Whitman said. "But [it had] a 70 percent compound monthly growth rate. Not compound annual [yearly] growth rate, compound *monthly* growth rate." In other words, each month the auction site operated, it earned 70 percent more revenue than the previous month.

Whitman saw that eBay offered users something that had never before existed—the ability to trade goods in a global marketplace 24 hours a day, seven days a week. It truly was a business that only could be conducted on

The eBay logo is one of the most recognizable logos on the internet.

the Internet. Whitman was even more impressed by the fact that users formed an emotional connection with eBay's service. She heard testimonials from users who would sneak away from business meetings to see how their auction was doing. She also heard about people who had discovered shared interests and become best friends by using the site. In short, people loved it. "For the past 20 years I had thought that great brands were features and functionality—you know, 'whiter whites' or 'cleaner cleans'—and if you can get the emotional connection, then you have a huge winner on your hands," she said. "There's no substitute in the land-based world for eBay. I just had an overwhelming instinct that this thing was going to be huge."

As excited as Whitman was about eBay, the company's founder and investors were even more excited to have her on board. Although she had no significant experience with technology, she did have extensive managerial, marketing, and brand experience. As Robert Kagle, a major eBay investor, explained, "I was looking for a brand-builder to help make eBay a household name."

When nearby Stanford University offered her husband a position as head of its neurosurgery department, Whitman felt as if "the stars aligned." She accepted a job as president and CEO of eBay in March 1998. A few years later, she reflected on her decision. "It was a huge risk. Sometimes my husband and I look back and say, 'What were we thinking?'" she acknowledged. "But we loved living in California and we thought that tech would continue to play an increasing role in society, and that being in the heartland of tech for us and our two boys would be positive. And we figured, what's the worst that could happen? I get another job."

Fitting into the eBay Culture

Even though most of her work experience had been at large corporations, Whitman fit right in at the fast-growing Internet start-up. She had no trouble giving up her fancy office and sharing a personal assistant with another manager. "My cubicle is the same size as the customer service reps'," she said. "You know, I don't actually miss the trappings of the offices I used to have. I love being in a smaller environment, feeling like I'm in a bit of a PT boat [a small, fast, maneuverable boat used to torpedo enemy ships in wartime], as opposed to a battleship."

> "There is always a lot of laughing in her office," said eBay founder Pierre Omidyar. "You know Meg is in a meeting when you hear her loud laughter."

In eBay's quick-changing environment, Whitman learned to think and act fast. In fact, she once estimated that in an average day at eBay she made the same number of decisions that would come up in two to three months at a more conventional company. "[It] is in many ways a different company every three months, and that's because the space is changing and the competitors are changing and the technology is changing so rapidly," she said. "In this space, the price of inaction is higher than the price of making a mistake."

Whitman worked closely with Omidyar during her first 18 months to really learn the business. "Side-by-side. Cubicle-by-cubicle," she noted. "I didn't make very many decisions without Pierre's input, and we just had a fabulous working relationship." Omidyar agreed, stating that "It's pretty rare that a founder [of a company] gets along so well with the new 'head of state' like Meg. There is always a lot of laughing in her office. You know Meg is in a meeting when you hear her loud laughter."

Taking eBay Public

One of Whitman's first duties as president and CEO of eBay was to prepare the company for its initial public offering (IPO) in September 1998. An IPO marks the first time that a corporation offers shares of stock for sale to investors on the public stock exchange. Many corporations stage an IPO, or "go public," as they grow in order to get money to pay for further expansion. Investors who purchased stock in eBay would become part-

Whitman poses with Pez candy dispensers during a photo session for a business magazine cover.

owners of the company. They would gain or lose money based on eBay's financial performance.

Prior to the offering, Whitman staged a nationwide eBay "road show." Joined by eBay's other top managers, she met with major investors to convince them that eBay was a good place to put their money. When the IPO finally took place, it was an overwhelming success. By the end of eBay's first day of trading on the stock exchange, its initial price of $18 per share had jumped to $47—an increase of 163 percent. By December 1998 the stock price went as high as $262.25 per share.

The rapid growth in eBay's stock price made Whitman one of the world's wealthiest business women. When she joined eBay in 1998, Whitman received options to buy 14.4 million shares of company stock at only 22 cents per share. A stock option is a common form of compensation that rewards top executives for increasing the price of the company's stock. Executives receive options to purchase shares at a low price, under the assumption that the stock price will go up over time. When they eventually exercise their option to purchase the shares, the executives can pocket the difference between the option price and the stock-market price on the day they are sold. Whitman sold 2.4 million of her shares in 1999 and 1.2 million in 2000. The selling prices ranged from $55 to more than $170 per share. As a result, Whitman's personal fortune has been estimated at between $700 million and $1.2 billion.

Improving eBay

Whitman made a number of improvements within a short time of her arrival at eBay. For example, she moved quickly to upgrade the eBay web site and to improve its look. She also launched a formal marketing plan. Within a year, celebrities were mentioning eBay in public and using the site to sell signed items for charity. As the site gained media attention, its customer base grew rapidly. By 2000 Whitman saw the number of eBay users increase from 750,000 to about 10 million. Two years later the number of registered users had swelled to 42 million, and more than $9 billion worth of merchandise was being traded on the site.

From the beginning, Whitman understood that users were the foundation of eBay's success. With that in mind, she has emphasized that all business decisions should be based on clear customer data. Customer surveys are routinely posted on the site, and many users' ideas have been adopted by the company over the years. The company has also sponsored live seminars around the country to help users make the most of eBay — and to encourage them to share their ideas about the site. Whitman also initiated a monthly "Voice of the Customer" day, when eBay brings a group of up to 20 users from around the world to its San Jose headquarters. The customers meet with eBay employees, including Whitman, to share their opinions, complaints, and ideas for improving eBay.

All of these innovations reflect Whitman's determination to make eBay users feel welcome and valued. "We started with commerce, and what grew out of that was community," Whitman explained. "The stories are myriad of people who really now do full time what they love to do, whether it's sell baseball cards or sell pottery, or whatever, because they can do it on eBay and make a living at what they love."

Whitman claims that eBay's emphasis on service and user satisfaction can be seen in every facet of the company's operations. For example, customers use the site's message boards to comment about fee increases, auction fraud, and other issues. And when Whitman makes a decision users do not like, they bombard her with hundreds of e-mail messages. "The great thing about running this company," she mused, "is that you know immediately what your customers think."

Facing Challenges

Of course, not all of Whitman's strategic decisions have proven successful. The company failed in an effort to establish a presence in the world of traditional auction houses. It also lost out to Yahoo! in a bid to capture the lucrative Japanese online auction market. But Whitman remained unfazed by these setbacks. "We have been careful to remain humble," she said. "We have to be free to say what we did didn't work and we'll try again."

> *"The stories are myriad of people who really now do full time what they love to do, whether it's sell baseball cards or sell pottery, or whatever, because they can do it on eBay and make a living at what they love," noted Whitman.*

One of the greatest challenges Whitman has faced at eBay occurred in 1999, when the eBay Internet site was shut down for 22 hours because of a system crash. Angry users swamped the site's technical support board with complaints. Whitman then closed the board entirely—a decision that her customers criticized. But Whitman earned back the trust of eBay users through her commitment to solving the technical problems. She worked 100 hours per week for a month—sleeping on a cot at the office—to make sure the outage was fixed. Company founder Pierre Omidyar called the incident "one of her shining moments. . . . Other executives might have said, 'I don't understand what's happening. Fix it.' Meg's response was to learn everything she possibly could learn." Eventually, eBay refunded millions of dollars to users who had listed items during the outage. The company also offered some users free auctions. Finally, Whitman ordered a major overhaul of the entire eBay network to ensure that the company and its users would be protected from future shut downs.

Whitman also moved decisively to address another major issue in eBay's business: auction fraud. Omidyar built the site on the premise that people

Whitman stands outside of eBay headquarters in San Jose, California.

are essentially trustworthy. The vast majority of eBay users, he believed, would deliver promised goods and make payments without a hitch. But as a precaution, he also established a message board. Sellers and buyers use the board to provide feedback about their dealings with each other. The site awards one point for a positive comment, zero points for a neutral comment, and minus one point for a negative comment. Users who reach a "minus-four" rating are barred from using eBay. Would-be users can easily access the comments and view the ratings.

In spite of this system, a small percentage of buyers and sellers still failed to deliver. Whitman responded by introducing a "comprehensive trust and safety program" at eBay. Sophisticated software analyzes buying and selling patterns to detect problems. The site offers users free insurance options for purchases up to $200. Customers also have the chance, for a small fee, to verify their identities with a credit-rating company. These measures have kept fraud to a manageable level on eBay.

Expanding eBay

In her five years at eBay, Whitman has won praise for her strategies for expanding the company. Under her leadership, eBay moved well beyond the collectibles, like Beanie Babies, that originally formed the core of the business. Now eBay moves virtually all types of goods—from nails to computer equipment. Different areas of the site are devoted to travel, sports, automobiles, and other types of goods. In addition, eBay has introduced dozens of regional Web sites for items like cars, boats, and other oversized goods that are hard to ship. Whitman also introduced specialty sites under the banner of eBay—much like individual shops housed within a big shopping mall.

In another innovation, Whitman helped move eBay beyond the auction-sale format. Inspired by Half.com—a Web site that offered fixed-price, discounted used merchandise—Whitman decided to offer eBay customers the option to buy goods right away, without an auction. A "Buy Now" button allows users to make a purchase at a set price. The "Buy Now" option proved so popular that it now accounts for about 30 percent of all purchases made on eBay.

In a further move to stimulate growth, Whitman encouraged companies and retail stores to trade on eBay. Both large corporations and small businesses now use the site to sell surplus goods or trade merchandise. Some of eBay's individual users expressed anger about big business moving onto the site. They feared that the larger companies would crowd them out or claim most of eBay's attention. Indeed, business experts warn that Whitman

"I think there's a minimum of 150,000 businesses that might not exist without eBay," claims Whitman.

will have to be careful not to alienate the individual users that have made eBay such a success. Thus far, however, eBay seems to be meeting the needs of all its users. As *Time* noted in 2003, "Mom-and-pop shops peddle their wares alongside IBM, Kodak, and Sears—and many stake their livelihood on the digital marketplace." Indeed, Whitman claims that "I think there's a minimum of 150,000 businesses that might not exist without eBay."

All of these initiatives have helped Whitman transform eBay into a worldwide presence. This expansion into overseas markets started early in her eBay career, when she acquired Europe's largest on-line auction site. She then moved aggressively to make a claim to a global marketplace. By early 2003 eBay either owned businesses or supported trading in about 30 countries. Revenues from this overseas trading grew by 173 percent in the last part of 2002. By mid-2003, eBay was valued at $32 billion, and it was estimated that it was handling transactions worth $59 million a day.

Looking ahead, Whitman acknowledges that eBay faces stiff competition from big Internet players like Yahoo! and Amazon.com, as well as at least 100 other online auction sites. But she claims that her biggest challenge involves attracting people to do business on the Internet. After all, most collectors and hobbyists still operate mainly through antique shops, trading fairs, or newspaper ads. "You know who our real competitor is? It's not the other online auction companies. It's the challenge of getting people to do on eBay what they do in the offline world," she acknowledged. "Our challenge is to get the offline transactions transferred online, because it's more efficient, more fun, and there's a bigger selection. Our real competitor is, in many ways, the old way of doing things."

> *"You know who our real competitor is?" said Whitman. "It's not the other online auction companies. It's the challenge of getting people to do on eBay what they do in the offline world. . . . Our real competitor is, in many ways, the old way of doing things."*

Success Makes Her a Celebrity

Whitman's management style and strategy won particular acclaim beginning in 2000. At a time when many Internet-based companies lost huge amounts of money or even failed, eBay continued to turn a profit. And its success has continued. In fact, eBay's earnings for the first three months of 2003 grew by 119 percent compared to a year earlier. A record 220 million listings appeared on the site from January through March. Much of the company's growth came from international markets, which provided 30 percent of eBay's revenues. "It seems like every business they touch, whether it be international or payments, they are able to grow it even further," said an industry analyst in 2003.

Whitman's high-profile success has made her a business celebrity and media favorite. She has appeared on magazine covers, television programs, and many lists of top business leaders. Although she does not reveal much about her personal life in interviews, many strangers treat her like a friend. "You know how you watch movies and you follow a star's career? You feel like you know them," she explained. "I think that is a little bit of what is going on now."

In spite of the unexpected burden of celebrity, Whitman loves her job. She particularly enjoys breaking ground in a brand-new marketplace. "It's really an interesting intellectual challenge — to figure out what the right thing to do is because there's really not a lot of 'best practices' to fall back on," she noted. Whitman also appreciates eBay's community of users. "It is incredibly fun to see entrepreneurs take advantage of this marketplace and utilize it in ways that we never would have dreamed of," she noted. Finally, Whitman says that she is happy to "build something that hasn't been done before on a global basis and have the company culture be the kind of company culture I always wanted to work in."

MARRIAGE AND FAMILY

Whitman married Griffith R. Harsh IV, a leading U.S. neurosurgeon, in 1980. They have two teenaged sons, Griff and Will. Whitman reportedly lives a relatively modest lifestyle. For example, she gets her wardrobe at department stores — but claims that she shops for clothes infrequently, because it bores her. Although she could easily afford a full staff at home, she employs only a cleaner. Her oldest son reportedly does most of the family's cooking. One of Whitman's biggest luxuries is avoiding work on the weekends. "Virtually all my time is dedicated to eBay and my family," Whitman said. "It's a wonderful life."

HOBBIES AND OTHER INTERESTS

In her spare time, Whitman enjoys skiing, tennis, and hiking. She and her family also like fly-fishing. "My 16-year-old son was very anxious to learn," Whitman said. "He loved it, and he said, 'Mom, you are going to love this.' We go five or six times a year." The family often spends vacations at her husband's family farm in Sweetwater, Tennessee, or in Colorado.

Whitman has shared her wealth to benefit others. She has given generously to her alma mater, Princeton University, where she sits on the board of trustees. In 2002 she promised $30 million to the university to establish a new residential college. The donation will allow Princeton to expand the number of students it serves and to provide financial help to attract applicants from a wider variety of social and economic backgrounds.

HONORS AND AWARDS

Third Most Powerful Woman in Business (*Fortune* magazine): 2002
Best CEOs (*Worth* Magazine): 2002
Top 25 Most Powerful Business Managers (*Business Week* magazine): 2000, 2001, 2002

FURTHER READING

Books

Bunnell, David, and Richard Luecke. *The eBay Phenomenon: Business Secrets Behind the World's Hottest Internet Company,* 2000
Business Leader Profiles for Students, Vol. 2, 2002
Cohen, Adam. *The Perfect Store: Inside eBay,* 2002

Periodicals

Atlanta Journal Constitution, June 6, 1999, p.H7
Business Week, Mar. 19, 2001, p.98
Current Biography Yearbook, 2002
Detroit Free Press, Apr. 3, 1995, p.F3
Fast Company, May 2001, p.72
Forbes, July 5, 1999, p.81; July 22, 2002, p.68
Fortune, Oct. 25, 1999, p.94; Jan. 21, 2002, p.78
Newsweek International, Oct. 11, 1999, p.50
New York Times, May 10, 1999, p.C1; May 5, 2002, p.L1
Time, Feb. 5, 2001, p.48; July 28, 2003, p.A9

Online Articles

http://business.cisco.com
    (Cisco Systems Online, "Q & A with eBay's Meg Whitman: The Charlie Rose Interview," July/Aug. 2001)

Online Databases

Biography Resource Center Online, 2003, articles from *Business Leader Profiles for Students,* 2002, and *Newsmakers 2000,* 2000

ADDRESS

Meg Whitman
eBay, Inc.
2125 Hamilton Ave.
San Jose, California 95125

WORLD WIDE WEB SITE

http://www.eBay.com

Yao Ming 1980-
Chinese Professional Basketball Player with the
Houston Rockets
First Overall Pick in the 2002 NBA Draft

BIRTH

Yao Ming was born on September 12, 1980, in Shanghai,
China. In Chinese practice, the family name comes before the
given name, so Yao is his family name (our last name) and
Ming is his given name (our first name). His hometown of
Shanghai is a busy commercial seaport on the East China Sea,
at the mouth of the Yangtze River. Yao's father, Yao Zhi Yuan, is

an engineering manager at the Shanghai harbor. His mother, Fang Feng Di, is an official in China's sports research institute. Both of Yao's parents played basketball for China's national teams in the 1970s. Yao, who is an only child, clearly inherited his height from his parents. His father stands six feet, seven inches tall, while his mother is six feet, three inches tall.

YOUTH AND EDUCATION

Yao grew up in a comfortable middle-class household in Shanghai. He was exceptionally tall even as a child, and his height affected many aspects of his youth. For example, Yao was as tall as his teacher in first grade. He also had to pay the full adult fare to ride public transportation. By the time he was 12 years old he had grown to six feet, six inches—a full foot taller than the average Chinese man. Yao's height eventually reached seven feet, five inches.

Yao's rapid growth left him feeling gawky and uncoordinated. As a boy, he was very thin and weak in the upper body. In fact, his friends jokingly referred to his arms as "chopsticks" because they were so skinny. Yao struggled in sports during this awkward phase. As a result, his first introduction to basketball proved embarrassing to him. When Yao was in the third grade, his teacher asked the class which student could shoot a basket from the free throw line. His classmates immediately suggested him. "This made me very proud at that time," he recalled, "but one of my classmates did better than me, and this remained a sore point for some time. Such was my first close contact with basketball."

When Yao was nine years old, Chinese government authorities selected him to attend the Shanghai Youth Sports School. Yao and his family had no choice but to obey the government's wishes. The People's Republic of China operates under a Communist form of government. Under this type of political system, the central government exercises a great deal of control over the lives of citizens. Communism eliminates most private property and gives it to the government to distribute as it sees fit. It also places severe restrictions on individual rights and allows the government to control the educations, careers, and cultural experiences of the people.

In an effort to build strong national sports teams to compete in the Olympic Games and other international competitions, China identifies potentially promising athletes at an early age. These young people are often taken from their families and sent away to elite sports training schools. Yao was selected for the Shanghai Youth Sports School on the basis of his height and his parents' successful athletic careers. He was initially placed on the water polo team at the school, but he soon switched to basketball. He received intensive training in basketball fundamentals from the school's coaches. He also worked on academics with a tutor for three hours per day and spent two hours each day studying on his own.

In 1994, at the age of 14, Yao was selected to join the Shanghai Youth Basketball Team. His skills improved quickly under the guidance of Coach Wang Qun. "At that time, I trained four times a day—a total of 10 hours," he recalled. "In order to help me master the basic skills, Mr. Wang was very strict. If I slackened my pace, he would punish me. . . . I could not be lazy under my coach's watchful eyes. According to the Chinese Basketball Association standard, I should be able to run 3,200 meters in 18 minutes, but with my coach's rigorous training, I can do it in 14 minutes." In the meantime, Yao continued his academic studies at the Shanghai Physical and Sport Technical Education Institute.

When Yao was in the third grade, his teacher asked the class which student could shoot a basket from the free throw line, and his classmates suggested him. "This made me very proud at the time," he recalled, "but one of my classmates did better than me, and this remained a sore point for some time. Such was my first close contact with basketball."

Yao's basketball talents first gained recognition outside of China in 1997, when he attended an elite basketball camp in France sponsored by Nike. During this competition against top young players from around the world, Yao learned new styles of play and improved his confidence. The following year Yao made his first trip to the United States, where he attended a series of high-profile basketball camps and clinics. He impressed NBA scouts at the Nike Junior Basketball Summer Camp by showing a rare combination of size, agility, intelligence, and outside shooting touch. Yao's excellent performances at these camps and clinics convinced him that he could make a career for himself in the NBA.

Despite his obvious talents, however, Yao still faced challenges in adapting to the American style of basketball. "When I went to America, I didn't like to dunk much," he remembered. "It's not the Chinese way. In America, I'd get the ball near the basket, shoot a layup, and the coach would be saying, 'Dunk the ball!' But I was used to laying it in. Finally,

Yao developed his basketball skills as a member of China's national team.

the coach said, 'If you get the ball in close and don't dunk it, all of your teammates are going to have to run laps.' But I couldn't help it. I was very accustomed to laying the ball in the basket. All of my teammates were running laps, begging me to dunk. Finally after about a week and many laps, I began to dunk it every time."

CAREER HIGHLIGHTS

Chinese Basketball Association: The Shanghai Sharks

Yao's professional basketball career began in 1997, when he joined the Shanghai Sharks of the Chinese Basketball Association (CBA). Basketball is very popular in China. The 12-team CBA attracted 130 million television viewers in China—as many people as typically watch the NFL Super Bowl in the United States—for regular-season games. Yao turned in a solid performance during his rookie CBA season, averaging 10 points and 8.3 rebounds per game. He also won the league's Sportsmanship Award. Unfortunately, the Sharks finished the season ranked eighth in the league.

In 1998 Yao suffered a broken foot and missed much of the CBA season. He came back strong in 1999, however, and improved his averages to 21.2 points and 14.5 rebounds per game.

——— *"* ———

"When I went to America, I didn't like to dunk much," Yao remembered. "Finally, the coach said, 'If you get the ball in close and don't dunk it, all of your teammates are going to have to run laps.' But I couldn't help it. I was very accustomed to laying the ball in the basket. All of my teammates were running laps, begging me to dunk. Finally after about a week and many laps, I began to dunk it every time."

——— *"* ———

By 2000 the 20-year-old Yao had developed into the most dominant player in the league. He averaged an impressive 27.1 points, 19.4 rebounds, and 5.5 blocked shots per game and was named the Most Valuable Player of the regular season. Led by their towering center, the Sharks advanced through the playoffs all the way to the CBA finals. But despite the best efforts of Yao and his teammates, the Sharks were defeated in the finals by the defending champion Bayi Rockets.

Yao posted another outstanding year in 2001. He led the CBA in blocked shots with 4.8 per game, and he ranked second in the league in both scoring (with 32.4 points per game) and rebounding (with 19 rebounds per game). The Sharks advanced to the CBA finals, where they again faced the Bayi Rockets. Yao dominated the championship series, posting 41.3 points, 21 rebounds, and 4.3 blocks per game. His strong performance lifted the Sharks to a 3-1 victory in the series and their first-ever CBA championship.

The Chinese National Team

China has long used its best professional basketball players to represent the country in international competition. Yao was selected to the Chinese National Team in 1998, at the age of 18. He trained with the team while he also continued to compete in the CBA with the Shanghai Sharks. In 2000 Yao played for the Chinese National Team at the Summer Olympic Games in Sydney, Australia.

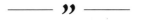

"I don't care if I'm the first Chinese player in the NBA or the second or the third. I just want to try it," Yao said.

The Chinese team's most anticipated game came early in the Olympic tournament, when they faced Team USA. Yao attracted a great deal of attention in the first few minutes of the game, dramatically swatting away shots by NBA stars Vince Carter and Gary Payton. But he eventually fouled out of the game, and the heavily favored American team coasted to a 119-72 victory. After the game, Yao expressed disappointment with his performance against the Americans. "Five minutes of playing well, or ten minutes, do not mean very much," he said afterward. "It's how well you play the entire game. One of American basketball's biggest strengths is understanding that. In the NBA, there are a lot of one-point and two-point games. There is intense competition to the final second."

During the Olympic tournament, Yao led the Chinese National Team in blocks (with 2.17 per game) and rebounds (with 6.0 per game), and he was second on the team in scoring (with 10.5 points per game). But China ended up finishing a disappointing tenth in the men's basketball competition, well out of medal contention. Some analysts claimed that this poor Olympic performance helped convince Chinese government officials to permit the country's star players to join the NBA, where they would gain needed experience against top competition.

In 2001 Yao helped the Chinese National Team capture the Asian Basketball Championship for Men and earn a spot in the World Championships.

He averaged 13.4 points, 10.1 rebounds, and 2.8 blocked shots per game and was named Most Valuable Player of the tournament. He was later named to the All-Tournament Team at the World Championships.

The Long Road to the NBA

Beginning in the late 1990s, NBA scouts kept a close eye on Yao's development as a basketball player. They hoped eventually to lure the young star to play in the NBA, which attracted many of the world's top players during the 1990s. In fact, by the 2001 season there were 45 international players competing on NBA teams. NBA officials also wanted to expand the league's recruiting base into China in order to attract Chinese fans. After all, China was the most populous nation in the world with 1.3 billion people. Around 200 million Chinese played basketball, and NBA games were already seen by 300 million Chinese on television. League officials believed that adding Chinese players to the rosters of NBA teams would dramatically increase the Chinese people's interest in the league.

Yao holds his new team jersey after the Houston Rockets selected him with the first pick of the 2002 NBA draft.

But some Chinese officials were reluctant to allow the country's top athletes to leave the country and play professionally in the United States. Under the Chinese sports system, Yao belonged to the Shanghai Sharks, the CBA, and the Chinese National Team. These entities had invested a great deal of time and money in training, feeding, housing, and educating Yao from the time he was nine years old. As a result, they felt that they should also benefit from his talents.

On the other hand, more progressive Chinese officials felt that the country would gain in the long run by sending its top athletes overseas to play against tougher competition. They wanted to show the world that China could develop basketball talent that could compete against the world's best. These feelings grew stronger following the Chinese National Team's disappointing performance in the 2000 Olympic Games. In 2001 China allowed two players to enter the NBA draft. Wang Zhi-Zhi, the seven-foot center of the Bayi Rockets, was drafted by the Dallas Mavericks, while another seven-footer, Mengke Bateer, went to the Denver Nuggets.

But the Shanghai Sharks refused to release Yao in 2001, so he could only watch as his teammates from the Chinese National Team left for the NBA. "I don't know if I'll be able to go or not, but I want to," he said at the time. "I don't care if I'm the first Chinese player in the NBA or the second or the third. I just want to try it." After the Sharks claimed the CBA title in 2001, team management said they would allow Yao to enter the NBA draft if the Chinese government agreed to let him leave the country.

Chinese officials recognized that Yao had the potential to earn millions of dollars in the NBA. They also realized that Yao's success would bring positive attention to China, which was hoping to host the 2008 Olympic Games in its capital city of Beijing. At the same time, however, they wanted to maintain some control over Yao's career. The Chinese government ultimately agreed to let Yao play in the NBA. But before he was allowed to leave the country, China published new rules that required Chinese athletes who competed professionally overseas to turn over half of their earnings — including income from advertising endorsements — to China for the length of their careers. The Chinese government also emphasized that it could recall its athletes at any time if they ignored the rules or if they were needed to represent China in international competition.

First Overall Pick in the 2002 NBA Draft

Shortly after receiving permission to play in the NBA, Yao was selected with the first overall pick in the 2002 NBA draft by the Houston Rockets. He thus became the third Chinese player in the NBA, and the first top draft pick ever taken from an international league. "I've waited so long for this," he said afterward. "Now I feel a real sense of peace that I've finally made it. But, I know there are many challenges ahead." Yao signed a four-year contract with the Rockets worth an estimated $18 million. He chose uniform number 11, which represents smoothness in Chinese culture.

Although Yao was thrilled to be the top overall pick in the draft, he recognized that this honor would not automatically make him a superstar in the

NBA. "Apart from [Allen] Iverson and [Tim] Duncan, few number one selections in the NBA draft have given an outstanding performance," he noted. "To improve my skills, I must set myself exacting targets. It doesn't matter whether I win the final championship or not. As long as I have tried my best, I will have no regrets."

Many basketball fans had high hopes that Yao would become the next great center in the NBA. The league had seen many of its star centers retire or reach the end of their careers in the late 1990s. By the time Yao was drafted, the only superstar centers playing in the NBA were Shaquille O'Neal of the Los Angeles Lakers and Tim Duncan of the San Antonio Spurs.

Yet some basketball fans doubted whether Yao would be able to make a successful adjustment to the NBA. They pointed out that the Chinese style of basketball—which emphasized teamwork over individual accomplishments—was very different from American basketball. In fact, the Chinese Basketball Association did not begin keeping track of statistics for individual players until 1995. Doubters also noted that Yao would have to deal with an unfamiliar language and culture. Finally, critics predicted that Yao would have trouble handling the pressure and media attention that would follow the first star Chinese player in the NBA.

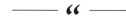

"To improve my skills, I must set myself exacting targets," declared Yao. "It doesn't matter whether I win the final championship or not. As long as I have tried my best, I will have no regrets."

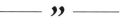

The Houston Rockets organization took a number of steps to help ease Yao's transition to the United States and the NBA. For example, they brought Yao's mother to Houston several weeks before he arrived. They gave her a tour of the city—including its many Chinese markets and restaurants—and helped her find a comfortable house to share with her son. Yao's father also visited for several weeks early in the season. The Rockets also hired an American, Colin Pine, to live with Yao and act as his translator and guide to American culture. Since Yao did not drive a car in China, the team presented him with a custom-made bicycle featuring an extra-large frame. Finally, the Rockets held a seminar to familiarize all team employees with Chinese cultural traditions.

During Yao's rookie season, he quickly emerged as a force on both the offensive and defensive ends of the court.

NBA: The Houston Rockets

The Rockets had finished the 2001-02 season with a 28-54 won-loss record, which earned the team fifth place in the Midwest Division of the NBA's Western Conference. The team's best player was point guard Steve Francis, nicknamed "The Franchise." The Rockets' starting lineup also included promising young guard Cuttino Mobley and forwards Glen Rice and Maurice Taylor. Many people anticipated that the addition of Yao would eventually help the Rockets become a playoff contender. But others worried that he would struggle to adapt to the NBA and become yet another disappointing high-profile draft pick.

Yao missed the Rockets' training camp and several preseason games because he was playing in the World Championships with the Chinese National Team. When he finally arrived in the United States, it did not take him long to earn the respect of his teammates with his solid fundamentals, hard work, and team-oriented attitude. "He's an incredibly endearing person. He's got this humble demeanor that is refreshing in our sport," said Houston Rockets general manager Carroll Dawson. "I remember the first day he came to practice. He missed all of training camp and most of our preseason because of obligations to his national team. There had been a tremendous amount of hype about him already, so I was curious to see how it went. In the first five minutes, he set three picks, made two terrific passes, and, when he scored, he ran back down the court with his head down. That's all it took. He had won his teammates over."

"I remember the first day [Yao] came to practice," recalled Houston general manager Carroll Dawson. "In the first five minutes, he set three picks, made two terrific passes, and, when he scored, he ran back down the court with his head down. That's all it took. He had won his teammates over."

Yao got off to a slow start once the 2002-03 NBA season began. He scored a total of 13 points in his first five games and sometimes looked a bit lost on the court. After all the attention that had surrounded his entering the league, some people seemed to take satisfaction in his early struggles. For example, the ESPN cable sports network put together a "lowlights" reel of Yao's worst moments on the court during his first week in the NBA. After one particularly poor outing, commentator and former NBA star Charles Barkley bet that Yao would never score 20 points in a game.

But Yao improved so quickly that he amazed many observers. He adapted to the NBA style of play and also adjusted to the constant attention he received from fans and the media. "I feel a lot of pressure on me," he admitted. "But I feel it every day. I am used to it. It is a bit of a burden on me, but I have to realize it's a responsibility I have to shoulder." Yao posted his first 20-point game less than a week after Barkley made his prediction. He scored a season-high 30 points a few weeks later against the Dallas Mavericks and their seven-foot, five-inch center, Shawn Bradley.

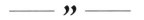

> "I feel a lot of pressure on me," admitted Yao. "But I feel it every day. I am used to it. It is a bit of a burden on me, but I have to realize it's a responsibility I have to shoulder."

Yao appeared in all 82 games during his rookie season with the Rockets, starting all but 10 games. He averaged a respectable 13.5 points, 8.2 rebounds, and 1.79 blocked shots per game. He achieved a season-high 19 rebounds in a game against Sacramento in March, and he blocked a season-high six shots in two different contests. Finally, Yao shot an impressive 81 percent from the free throw line. He ended up finishing a close second behind Amare Stoudemire of the Phoenix Suns for NBA Rookie of the Year honors.

Rockets fans and management were thrilled with the solid performance of the team's top draft pick. "People ask me all the time if I'm surprised Yao is this good," said Rockets general manager Carroll Dawson. "The answer is no. I knew he'd be this good. We've been following him since he was 15. But I had no idea he'd be this good this fast." For his part, Yao credited Rockets Coach Rudy Tomjanovich and his teammates for his easy transition to the NBA. "I don't know what happened," he stated. "It's a testament to my coaches and teammates. They've helped me very much."

Boosted by Yao's intimidating presence in the middle, the Rockets won 15 more games than they had the season before. He also helped transform Houston into one of the league's most exciting teams. But despite finishing the season with a 43-39 won-loss record, the Rockets failed to qualify for a berth in the NBA playoffs.

At season's end, Yao's mother expressed great pride in her son's accomplishments. "Yao Ming was coming to a completely new environment, an environment completely different from China," she noted. "He never had any NBA experience or much experience in the United States. He had none of the experience of American basketball. And of course, there are differences between basketball in China and the U.S. Before he was playing by international rules, not NBA rules. He's not as big and strong as the American players. I thought there would be a longer period of adjustment for him."

The Start of a Rivalry

As the 2002-03 NBA season progressed and Yao showed rapid improvement, basketball fans eagerly anticipated the first matchup between him and Shaquille O'Neal. The Rockets did not face the defending NBA champion Los Angeles Lakers until January 2003, but O'Neal apparently grew tired of being compared to Yao long before that. When yet another reporter asked the Lakers' star center about the Rockets' rookie center, O'Neal adopted a fake Chinese accent and said, "Tell Yao Ming, 'Ching chong yang wah ah so.'"

NBA observers believe that Yao is one of the few players capable of challenging Los Angeles Lakers center Shaquille O'Neal for recognition as the league's top center.

O'Neal's remark created a controversy. Many people, including members of prominent Asian-American organizations, criticized him for showing a lack of sensitivity toward Chinese culture. But Yao refused to take offense and instead chose to handle the situation diplomatically. When a reporter asked Yao about his rival's remark, Yao joked that Chinese was a difficult language to learn. When the Lakers came to Houston, Yao invited O'Neal to his house for dinner (Shaq had to decline the invitation due to a previous engagement with his daughter). Yao later explained the reason behind his calm reaction to the controversy. "Chinese people don't want other people to lose face," he said. "In Chinese culture, you will be looked down on just for letting someone lose face."

When the two big men finally faced off against each other on the court, O'Neal tested Yao immediately with a series of post-up moves near the basket. Yao responded by swatting away three of O'Neal's shots within the first few minutes of the game. The Lakers' star went on to have an impressive night, with 31 points and 13 rebounds. By contrast, Yao only managed 10 points and 10 rebounds. Nonetheless, many observers felt that a rivalry emerged between the big men during the course of the game. After all, Yao blocked O'Neal's shot five times during the game. Until that time, opponents had only managed to block O'Neal once every other game during the season. Most important of all, Yao's performance helped the Rockets defeat the Lakers 108-104 in overtime.

"[Yao's] a really bright guy, and he understands a lot," said his translator. *"But he is not fluent [in English] by any means. Imagine if you were dropped into China and had three months to learn the language. Do you think you'd be ready to conduct a press conference?"*

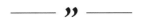

A few weeks later, Yao easily beat O'Neal in total fan votes to become the starting center for the Western Conference in the NBA All-Star Game. Yao was excited about appearing in the All-Star Game, but he insisted that he did not deserve to start over O'Neal. "He's the best center in the game," Yao said of Shaq. "Why can't he start and I come off the bench?" In fact, Yao claimed that he needed to improve his upper-body strength, rebounding skills, and reaction time on defense in order to better compete with O'Neal and other NBA stars.

Brings Excitement and an International Audience to the NBA

Throughout his first NBA season, Yao attracted hordes of new fans to the game of basketball. The excitement surrounding his selection in the draft helped the Rockets draw sellout crowds for home games for the first time since 1999. But Yao's appeal was not limited to Houston. People from across the United States also flocked to see Yao play when the Rockets went on road trips. Fans everywhere appreciated his playing skills, humble attitude, solid work ethic, and sense of humor.

Yao's celebrity status has given him opportunities to meet other famous athletes, such as tennis star Andre Agassi.

As the season progressed, Yao also emerged as a particular source of pride for people of Chinese descent. In fact, live broadcasts of Rockets games—which aired early in the morning—attracted 5.5 million viewers in China. Another 11.5 million people tuned in when the games were rebroadcast later in the day. In comparison, an average weeknight telecast of an NBA game drew only 1.1 million viewers in the United States. Some experts have said that if Yao has a successful NBA career, he could become the best-known athlete in the world.

Yao's popularity has already earned him several high-profile endorsement deals. He appeared in television commercials for Visa credit cards and Apple laptop computers, for example, and in a print advertisement for the Got Milk? campaign. In addition, Yao's endorsement opportunities are expected to increase as his English language skills improve. Although he knows enough basketball terms to understand his teammates and converse with them on the court, he still uses an interpreter when speaking with the media. "He is a really bright guy, and he understands a lot," said his translator, Colin Pine. "But he is not fluent by any means. Imagine if you were dropped into China and had three months to learn the language. Do you think you'd be ready to conduct a press conference?" "I still don't understand a lot of things," Yao admitted. "If I did, you would have been fired a while ago," he joked with his translator.

Yao, who has gained such nicknames as "The Little Giant" and "The Great Wall," understands that he represents China in the minds of many basketball fans. "I'm not the only thing that is exciting about China," he noted. "There are a lot of things about China that are exciting. I'm just doing what I always do and doing what I think I should do. I don't think it's a burden. But if people can learn something from that, that's great."

Although he earns millions of dollars and is recognized by fans around the world, Yao claims that he still plays basketball for the love of the game. "Every sound in the gym is so fantastic," he stated. "The screams of the fans, the whistle of the ref, the teammates calling to each other, the sounds of the ball touching the wooden floor, the sneakers touching the floor, and the sounds of the fight, the muscle and the sweat. Oh, and the last one—when the ball goes through the net. Don't laugh at my sensitivity and romanticism, those sounds really attract me."

HOME AND FAMILY

During the NBA season, Yao lives in a four-bedroom house in the Houston suburbs. He shares his home with his interpreter, Colin Pine, and his mother, who stayed in the United States to help ease his adjustment during his rookie year. "I want to give him support," she explained. "I want to be able to provide a place where he can feel at home, so that when he has worries outside, when he comes back, he has something to rely on. I think a good mother and a good father can do that. I worry about him. I see the pressure." Yao appreciates his parents' support, and especially his mother's home cooking. "The fact that my parents are here has made my adjustment to American life much easier," he acknowledged, "although really there hasn't been anything that difficult to get adjusted to."

Yao is not married, but he does have a long-distance girlfriend, Ye Li. She is a six-foot, three-inch basketball player for the Chinese Women's National Team. Yao always wears a red string bracelet that he received as a gift from her.

HOBBIES AND OTHER INTERESTS

In his spare time, Yao enjoys playing computer games and fishing. "I like to fish," he said. "But the fish don't pay attention to me." Yao also likes studying Chinese history, especially stories about the ancient leader Zhu Ge-Liang, who was known for his brilliant strategy.

—— " ——

"Every sound in the gym is so fantastic," said Yao. "The screams of the fans, the whistle of the ref, the teammates calling to each other, the sounds of the ball touching the wooden floor, the sneakers touching the floor, and the sounds of the fight, the muscle and the sweat. Oh, and the last one—when the ball goes through the net. Don't laugh at my sensitivity and romanticism, those sounds really attract me."

—— " ——

HONORS AND AWARDS

Sportsmanship Award (Chinese Basketball Association): 1997
Most Valuable Player (Chinese Basketball Association): 2000
Chinese Basketball Association Championship: 2001, with Shanghai
    Sharks
Next Athlete (*ESPN The Magazine*): 2001
Most Valuable Player (Asian Basketball Championship
    for Men): 2001
First Overall Selection in the NBA Draft: 2002, by Houston Rockets
NBA All-Star Game: 2002-03 (starting center, Western Conference)

FURTHER READING

Periodicals

Boston Globe, Jan. 16, 1999, p.A1; Jan. 13, 2003, p.D1
ESPN The Magazine, Feb. 17, 2003, p.43
Houston Chronicle, Oct. 15, 2002, Sports sec., p.9; Oct. 20, 2002, Sports sec.,
    p.1; Dec. 25, 2002, Sports sec., p.1
Los Angeles Times, Nov. 17, 2002, Sports sec., p.1
New York Times, Apr. 25, 2002, p.A1; Nov. 2, 2002, p.D1; Dec. 15, 2002,
    Sports sec., p.1; Jan. 18, 2003, p.D1; Feb. 8, 2003, p.D4
Newsday, Feb. 9, 2003, p.B14
Newsweek International, Apr. 10, 2000, p.69; Apr. 30, 2001, p.12
Sporting News, Sep. 9, 2002, p.54; Jan. 20, 2003, p.6
Sports Illustrated, Sep. 11, 2000, p.148; May 13, 2002, p.86; Oct. 28, 2002,
    p.66; Jan. 27, 2003, p.58
Sports Illustrated for Kids, May 2003, p.25
Time, Feb. 10, 2003, p.68
USA Today, Oct. 29, 2002, p.A1
Wall Street Journal, Feb. 11, 1999, p.A24
Washington Post, Dec. 13, 2002, p.A1

Online Articles

http://espn.go.com/magazine/vol3no26ming.html
    (*ESPN The Magazine,* "Next Athlete: Yao Ming," Dec. 25, 2000)
http://www.chinatoday.com.cn/English/e20029/yao.htm
    (*China Today,* "Yao Ming: The Chinese NBA Player," Sep. 2002)

ADDRESS

Yao Ming
Houston Rockets
Compaq Center
10 Greenway Plaza East
Houston, TX 77046

WORLD WIDE WEB SITES

http://www.yaoming.net
http://www.nba.com/

Photo and Illustration Credits

Vincent Brooks/Photos: AP/Wide World Photos. Front Cover: copyright © Tim Aubry/Reuters/Landov

Amanda Bynes/Photos: copyright © The WB/James Sorenson; Stephen Osman/Los Angeles Times/Retna; copyright © The WB/Ron Batzdorff; Kevin Winter/Getty Images; What a Girl Wants copyright © 2003 Warner Brothers; DVD cover: courtesy of Universal Studios Home Video.

Josh Hartnett/Photos: Ethan Miller/Reuters; Rico Torres; Newscom.com; AP/Wide World Photos; Black Hawk Down © Columbia TriStar Marketing Group, Inc. All rights reserved; Sidney Baldwin; AP/Wide World Photos.

Dolores Huerta/Photos: Walter P. Reuther Library, Wayne State University; Arthur Schatz/Time Life Pictures/Getty Images; Walter P. Reuther Library, Wayne State University; AP/Wide World Photos.

Nicklas Lidstrom/Photos: AP/Wide World Photos; Elsa Hasch/Getty Images; AP/Wide World Photos; Elsa Hasch/Getty Images/NHLI.

Nelly/Photos: AP/Wide World Photos; copyright © Paul Smith/Feature flash/Retna; Frank Micelotta/Getty Images; Kevin Winter/Getty Images; copyright © Thorsten Buhe/Vanit/Retna. CD covers: *Country Grammar* (p) © 2000 Universal Records, a division of UMG Recordings, Inc.; *Nellyville* (p) © 2002 Universal Records, a division of UMG Recordings, Inc.

Gwen Stefani/Photos: Donald Miralle/Getty Images; copyright © Los Angeles Times/Retna; copyright © Tara Canova/Retna; AP/Wide World Photos; Newscom.com. CD covers: *Rock Steady* (p) © 2001 Interscope Records; *Tragic Kingdom* © 1995 Interscope Records.

Margaret Whitman/Photos: AP/Wide World Photos; Newscom.com.

Yao Ming/Photos: Peter Jones/Reuters/Landov; AP/Wide World Photos; Alex Livesey/Getty Images; AP/Wide World Photos. Cover: AP/Wide World Photos.

How to Use the Cumulative Index

Our indexes have a new look. In an effort to make our indexes easier to use, we've combined the Name and General Index into a new, Cumulative Index. This single ready-reference resource covers all the volumes in *Biography Today,* both the general series and the special subject series. The new Cumulative Index contains complete listings of all individuals who have appeared in *Biography Today* since the series began. Their names appear in bold-faced type, followed by the issue in which they appear. The Cumulative Index also includes references for the occupations, nationalities, and ethnic and minority origins of individuals profiled in *Biography Today.*

We have also made some changes to our specialty indexes, the Places of Birth Index and the Birthday Index. To consolidate and to save space, the Places of Birth Index and the Birthday Index will no longer appear in the January and April issues of the softbound subscription series. But these indexes can still be found in the September issue of the softbound subscription series, in the hardbound Annual Cumulation at the end of each year, and in each volume of the special subject series.

General Series

The General Series of *Biography Today* is denoted in the index with the month and year of the issue in which the individual appeared. Each individual also appears in the Annual Cumulation for that year.

Special Subject Series

The Special Subject Series of *Biography Today* are each denoted in the index with an abbreviated form of the series name, plus the number of the volume in which the individual appears. They are listed as follows.

Adams, Ansel .... Artist V.1   (Artists)
Flake, Sharon. .... Author V.13   (Authors)
Jackson, Peter .... PerfArt V.2   (Performing Artists)
Kapell, Dave .... Science V.8   (Scientists & Inventors)
Kidd, Jason .... Sport V.9   (Sports)
Peterson, Roger Tory .... WorLdr V.1   (World Leaders: Environmental Leaders)
Sadat, Anwar .... WorLdr V.2   (World Leaders: Modern African Leaders)
Wolf, Hazel. .... WorLdr V.3   (World Leaders: Environmental Leaders 2)

Updates

Updated information on selected individuals appears in the Appendix at the end of the *Biography Today* Annual Cumulation. In the index, the original entry is listed first, followed by any updates.

Arafat, Yasir .... Sep 94; Update 94; Update 95; Update 96; Update 97; Update 98; Update 00; Update 01; Update 02
Gates, Bill .... Apr 93; Update 98; Update 00; Science V.5; Update 01
Griffith Joyner, Florence. .... Sport V.1; Update 98
Sanders, Barry .... Sep 95; Update 99
Spock, Dr. Benjamin .... Sep 95; Update 98
Yeltsin, Boris .... Apr 92; Update 93; Update 95; Update 96; Update 98; Update 00

Cumulative Index

This cumulative index includes names, occupations, nationalities, and ethnic and minority origins that pertain to all individuals profiled in *Biography Today* since the debut of the series in 1992.

autobiographies

ballet
    see dance
Barr, Roseanne
baseball

basketball

Pope of the Roman Catholic Church

Portman, Natalie
Potter, Beatrix
Powell, Colin
Prelutsky, Jack
presidents
– Cuba
– Egypt
– Ghana
– Haiti
– Iraq
– Ireland
– Kenya
– Liberia
– Malawi
– Republic of South Africa

tennis

Places of Birth Index

The following index lists the places of birth for the individuals profiled in *Biography Today*. Places of birth are entered under state, province, and/or country.

203

Ethiopia

Haile Selassie – *Ejarsa Goro,*
Harar . . . . WorLdr V.2
Roba, Fatuma – *Bokeji* . . . . Sport V.3

Florida

Carter, Aaron – *Tampa* . . . . Sep 02
Carter, Vince – *Daytona Beach* . . . . Sport V.5
Dorough, Howie – *Orlando* . . . . Jan 00
Evert, Chris – *Ft. Lauderdale* . . . . . Sport V.1
Griese, Brian – *Miami* . . . . Jan 02
McLean, A.J. – *West Palm Beach* . . . . . Jan 00
Reno, Janet – *Miami* . . . . Sep 93
Richardson, Dot – *Orlando* . . . . . . Sport V.2
Robinson, David – *Key West* . . . . Sep 96
Rubin, Jamie – *Fort Myers* . . . . . Science V.8
Sanders, Deion – *Ft. Myers* . . . . . . Sport V.1
Sapp, Warren – *Plymouth* . . . . Sport V.5
Smith, Emmitt – *Pensacola* . . . . Sep 94
Tarvin, Herbert – *Miami* . . . . Apr 97

France

Córdova, France – *Paris* . . . . Science V.7
Cousteau, Jacques – *St. Andre-de-*
Cubzac . . . . Jan 93
Ma, Yo-Yo – *Paris* . . . . Jul 92
Marceau, Marcel – *Strasbourg* . . PerfArt V.2

Georgia

Carter, Jimmy – *Plains* . . . . Apr 95
Grant, Amy – *Augusta* . . . . Jan 95
Hogan, Hulk – *Augusta* . . . . Apr 92
Johns, Jasper – *Augusta* . . . . Artist V.1
Lee, Spike – *Atlanta* . . . . Apr 92
Mathis, Clint – *Conyers* . . . . Apr 03
Roberts, Julia – *Atlanta* . . . . Sep 01
Robinson, Jackie – *Cairo* . . . . Sport V.3
Rowland, Kelly – *Atlanta* . . . . Apr 01
Thomas, Clarence – *Pin Point* . . . . Jan 92
Tucker, Chris – *Decatur* . . . . Jan 01
Ward, Charlie – *Thomasville* . . . . Apr 94

Germany

Bethe, Hans A. – *Strassburg* . . . . Science V.3
Frank, Anne – *Frankfort* . . . . Author V.4
Galdikas, Biruté – *Wiesbaden* . . . Science V.4
Graf, Steffi – *Mannheim* . . . . Jan 92
Otto, Sylke – *Karl-Marx Stad*
(Chemnitz) . . . . Sport V.8
Pippig, Uta – *Berlin* . . . . Sport V.1

Ghana

Annan, Kofi – *Kumasi* . . . . Jan 98
Nkrumah, Kwame – *Nkrofro* . . . WorLdr V.2

Guatemala

Menchu, Rigoberta – *Chimel,*
El Quiche . . . . Jan 93

Haiti

Aristide, Jean-Bertrand – *Port-Salut* . . . Jan 95

Hawaii

Case, Steve – *Honolulu* . . . . Science V.5
Lowry, Lois – *Honolulu* . . . . Author V.4
Nakamura, Leanne – *Honolulu* . . . . . Apr 02
Tuttle, Merlin – *Honolulu* . . . . Apr 97
Yelas, Jay – *Honolulu* . . . . Sport V.9

Holland

Lionni, Leo –
Watergraafsmeer . . . . Author V.6

Hungary

Erdös, Paul – *Budapest* . . . . Science V.2

Idaho

Street, Picabo – *Triumph* . . . . Sport V.3

Illinois

Anderson, Gillian – *Chicago* . . . . Jan 97
Bauer, Joan – *River Forest* . . . . . Author V.10
Blackmun, Harry – *Nashville* . . . . Jan 00
Blum, Deborah – *Urbana* . . . . Science V.8
Boyd, Candy Dawson – *Chicago* . Author V.3
Bradbury, Ray – *Waukegan* . . . . . Author V.3
Clinton, Hillary Rodham – *Chicago* . . Apr 93
Crawford, Cindy – *De Kalb* . . . . Apr 93
Crichton, Michael – *Chicago* . . . . Author V.5
Cushman, Karen – *Chicago* . . . . Author V.5
Ford, Harrison – *Chicago* . . . . Sep 97
Garth, Jennie – *Urbana* . . . . Apr 96
Gorey, Edward – *Chicago* . . . . . Author V.13
Granato, Cammi –
Downers Grove . . . . Sport V.8
Hansberry, Lorraine – *Chicago* . . Author V.5
Hendrickson, Sue – *Chicago* . . . Science V.7
Jones, Quincy – *Chicago* . . . . PerfArt V.2
Joyner-Kersee, Jackie – *East*
St. Louis . . . . Oct 92
Mac, Bernie – *Chicago* . . . . PerfArt V.1
Margulis, Lynn – *Chicago* . . . . Sep 96
McCully, Emily Arnold – *Galesburg* . . Jul 92
McGruder, Aaron – *Chicago* . . . Author V.10
McNabb, Donovan – *Chicago* . . . . . . Apr 03
Park, Linda Sue – *Urbana* . . . . . Author V.12
Peck, Richard – *Decatur* . . . . . . Author V.10
Silverstein, Shel – *Chicago* . . . . . Author V.3
Siskel, Gene – *Chicago* . . . . Sep 99
Van Draanen, Wendelin –
Chicago . . . . Author V.11
Watson, James D. – *Chicago* . . . Science V.1
Williams, Michelle – *Rockford* . . . . . Apr 01
Wrede, Patricia C. – *Chicago* . . . Author V.7

Birthday Index

Biography Today

General Series

Biography Today **General Series** includes a unique combination of current biographical profiles that teachers and librarians — and the readers themselves — tell us are most appealing. The **General Series** is available as a 3-issue subscription; hardcover annual cumulation; or subscription plus cumulation.

Within the **General Series**, your readers will find a variety of sketches about:

- Authors
- Musicians
- Political leaders
- Sports figures
- Movie actresses & actors
- Cartoonists
- Scientists
- Astronauts
- TV personalities
- and the movers & shakers in many other fields!

"Biography Today will be useful in elementary and middle school libraries and in public library children's collections where there is a need for biographies of current personalities. High schools serving reluctant readers may also want to consider a subscription."

— *Booklist,* American Library Association

"Highly recommended for the young adult audience. Readers will delight in the accessible, energetic, tell-all style; teachers, librarians, and parents will welcome the clever format, intelligent and informative text. It should prove especially useful in motivating 'reluctant' readers or literate nonreaders."

— *MultiCultural Review*

"Written in a friendly, almost chatty tone, the profiles offer quick, objective information. While coverage of current figures makes *Biography Today* a useful reference tool, an appealing format and wide scope make it a fun resource to browse." — *School Library Journal*

"The best source for current information at a level kids can understand."
— Kelly Bryant, School Librarian, Carlton, OR

"Easy for kids to read. We love it! Don't want to be without it."
— Lynn McWhirter, School Librarian, Rockford, IL

ONE-YEAR SUBSCRIPTION
- 3 softcover issues, 6" x 9"
- Published in January, April, and September
- 1-year subscription, $60
- 150 pages per issue
- 8-10 profiles per issue
- Contact sources for additional information
- Cumulative General, Places of Birth, and Birthday Indexes

HARDBOUND ANNUAL CUMULATION
- Sturdy 6" x 9" hardbound volume
- Published in December
- $62 per volume
- 450 pages per volume
- 25-30 profiles — includes all profiles found in softcover issues for that calendar year
- Cumulative General, Places of Birth, and Birthday Indexes
- Special appendix features current updates of previous profiles

SUBSCRIPTION AND CUMULATION COMBINATION
- $99 for 3 softcover issues plus the hardbound volume

1992

Paula Abdul
Andre Agassi
Kirstie Alley
Terry Anderson
Roseanne Arnold
Isaac Asimov
James Baker
Charles Barkley
Larry Bird
Judy Blume
Berke Breathed
Garth Brooks
Barbara Bush
George Bush
Fidel Castro
Bill Clinton
Bill Cosby
Diana, Princess of Wales
Shannen Doherty
Elizabeth Dole
David Duke
Gloria Estefan
Mikhail Gorbachev
Steffi Graf
Wayne Gretzky
Matt Groening
Alex Haley
Hammer
Martin Handford
Stephen Hawking
Hulk Hogan
Saddam Hussein
Lee Iacocca
Bo Jackson
Mae Jemison
Peter Jennings
Steven Jobs
Pope John Paul II
Magic Johnson
Michael Jordon
Jackie Joyner-Kersee
Spike Lee
Mario Lemieux
Madeleine L'Engle
Jay Leno
Yo-Yo Ma
Nelson Mandela
Wynton Marsalis
Thurgood Marshall
Ann Martin
Barbara McClintock
Emily Arnold McCully
Antonia Novello

Sandra Day O'Connor
Rosa Parks
Jane Pauley
H. Ross Perot
Luke Perry
Scottie Pippen
Colin Powell
Jason Priestley
Queen Latifah
Yitzhak Rabin
Sally Ride
Pete Rose
Nolan Ryan
H. Norman
   Schwarzkopf
Jerry Seinfeld
Dr. Seuss
Gloria Steinem
Clarence Thomas
Chris Van Allsburg
Cynthia Voigt
Bill Watterson
Robin Williams
Oprah Winfrey
Kristi Yamaguchi
Boris Yeltsin

1993

Maya Angelou
Arthur Ashe
Avi
Kathleen Battle
Candice Bergen
Boutros Boutros-Ghali
Chris Burke
Dana Carvey
Cesar Chavez
Henry Cisneros
Hillary Rodham Clinton
Jacques Cousteau
Cindy Crawford
Macaulay Culkin
Lois Duncan
Marian Wright Edelman
Cecil Fielder
Bill Gates
Sara Gilbert
Dizzy Gillespie
Al Gore
Cathy Guisewite
Jasmine Guy
Anita Hill
Ice-T
Darci Kistler

k.d. lang
Dan Marino
Rigoberta Menchu
Walter Dean Myers
Martina Navratilova
Phyllis Reynolds Naylor
Rudolf Nureyev
Shaquille O'Neal
Janet Reno
Jerry Rice
Mary Robinson
Winona Ryder
Jerry Spinelli
Denzel Washington
Keenen Ivory Wayans
Dave Winfield

1994

Tim Allen
Marian Anderson
Mario Andretti
Ned Andrews
Yasir Arafat
Bruce Babbitt
Mayim Bialik
Bonnie Blair
Ed Bradley
John Candy
Mary Chapin Carpenter
Benjamin Chavis
Connie Chung
Beverly Cleary
Kurt Cobain
F.W. de Klerk
Rita Dove
Linda Ellerbee
Sergei Fedorov
Zlata Filipovic
Daisy Fuentes
Ruth Bader Ginsburg
Whoopi Goldberg
Tonya Harding
Melissa Joan Hart
Geoff Hooper
Whitney Houston
Dan Jansen
Nancy Kerrigan
Alexi Lalas
Charlotte Lopez
Wilma Mankiller
Shannon Miller
Toni Morrison
Richard Nixon
Greg Norman
Severo Ochoa

River Phoenix
Elizabeth Pine
Jonas Salk
Richard Scarry
Emmitt Smith
Will Smith
Steven Spielberg
Patrick Stewart
R.L. Stine
Lewis Thomas
Barbara Walters
Charlie Ward
Steve Young
Kim Zmeskal

1995

Troy Aikman
Jean-Bertrand Aristide
Oksana Baiul
Halle Berry
Benazir Bhutto
Jonathan Brandis
Warren E. Burger
Ken Burns
Candace Cameron
Jimmy Carter
Agnes de Mille
Placido Domingo
Janet Evans
Patrick Ewing
Newt Gingrich
John Goodman
Amy Grant
Jesse Jackson
James Earl Jones
Julie Krone
David Letterman
Rush Limbaugh
Heather Locklear
Reba McEntire
Joe Montana
Cosmas Ndeti
Hakeem Olajuwon
Ashley Olsen
Mary-Kate Olsen
Jennifer Parkinson
Linus Pauling
Itzhak Perlman
Cokie Roberts
Wilma Rudolph
Salt 'N' Pepa
Barry Sanders
William Shatner
Elizabeth George
   Speare

Dr. Benjamin Spock
Jonathan Taylor
Thomas
Vicki Van Meter
Heather Whitestone
Pedro Zamora

1996

Aung San Suu Kyi
Boyz II Men
Brandy
Ron Brown
Mariah Carey
Jim Carrey
Larry Champagne III
Christo
Chelsea Clinton
Coolio
Bob Dole
David Duchovny
Debbi Fields
Chris Galeczka
Jerry Garcia
Jennie Garth
Wendy Guey
Tom Hanks
Alison Hargreaves
Sir Edmund Hillary
Judith Jamison
Barbara Jordan
Annie Leibovitz
Carl Lewis
Jim Lovell
Mickey Mantle
Lynn Margulis
Iqbal Masih
Mark Messier
Larisa Oleynik
Christopher Pike
David Robinson
Dennis Rodman
Selena
Monica Seles
Don Shula
Kerri Strug
Tiffani-Amber Thiessen
Dave Thomas
Jaleel White

1997

Madeleine Albright
Marcus Allen
Gillian Anderson
Rachel Blanchard
Zachery Ty Bryan
Adam Ezra Cohen
Claire Danes
Celine Dion
Jean Driscoll
Louis Farrakhan
Ella Fitzgerald
Harrison Ford
Bryant Gumbel
John Johnson
Michael Johnson
Maya Lin
George Lucas
John Madden
Bill Monroe
Alanis Morissette
Sam Morrison
Rosie O'Donnell
Muammar el-Qaddafi
Christopher Reeve
Pete Sampras
Pat Schroeder
Rebecca Sealfon
Tupac Shakur
Tabitha Soren
Herbert Tarvin
Merlin Tuttle
Mara Wilson

1998

Bella Abzug
Kofi Annan
Neve Campbell
Sean Combs (Puff
Daddy)
Dalai Lama (Tenzin
Gyatso)
Diana, Princess of Wales
Leonardo DiCaprio
Walter E. Diemer
Ruth Handler
Hanson
Livan Hernandez
Jewel
Jimmy Johnson
Tara Lipinski
Jody-Anne Maxwell
Dominique Moceanu
Alexandra Nechita

Brad Pitt
LeAnn Rimes
Emily Rosa
David Satcher
Betty Shabazz
Kordell Stewart
Shinichi Suzuki
Mother Teresa
Mike Vernon
Reggie White
Kate Winslet

1999

Ben Affleck
Jennifer Aniston
Maurice Ashley
Kobe Bryant
Bessie Delany
Sadie Delany
Sharon Draper
Sarah Michelle Gellar
John Glenn
Savion Glover
Jeff Gordon
David Hampton
Lauryn Hill
King Hussein
Lynn Johnston
Shari Lewis
Oseola McCarty
Mark McGwire
Slobodan Milosevic
Natalie Portman
J. K. Rowling
Frank Sinatra
Gene Siskel
Sammy Sosa
John Stanford
Natalia Toro
Shania Twain
Mitsuko Uchida
Jesse Ventura
Venus Williams

2000

Christina Aguilera
K.A. Applegate
Lance Armstrong
Backstreet Boys
Daisy Bates
Harry Blackmun
George W. Bush
Carson Daly
Ron Dayne
Henry Louis Gates, Jr.
Doris Haddock
(Granny D)
Jennifer Love Hewitt
Chamique Holdsclaw
Katie Holmes
Charlayne Hunter-Gault
Johanna Johnson
Craig Kielburger
John Lasseter
Peyton Manning
Ricky Martin
John McCain
Walter Payton
Freddie Prinze, Jr.
Viviana Risca
Briana Scurry
George Thampy
CeCe Winans

2001

Jessica Alba
Christiane Amanpour
Drew Barrymore
Jeff Bezos
Destiny's Child
Dale Earnhardt
Carly Fiorina
Aretha Franklin
Cathy Freeman
Tony Hawk
Faith Hill
Kim Dae-jung
Madeleine L'Engle
Mariangela Lisanti
Frankie Muniz
*N Sync
Ellen Ochoa
Jeff Probst
Julia Roberts
Carl T. Rowan
Britney Spears
Chris Tucker
Lloyd D. Ward
Alan Webb
Chris Weinke

2002

Aaliyah
Osama bin Laden
Mary J. Blige
Aubyn Burnside
Aaron Carter
Julz Chavez
Dick Cheney
Hilary Duff
Billy Gilman
Rudolph Giuliani
Brian Griese
Jennifer Lopez
Dave Mirra
Dineh Mohajer
Leanne Nakamura
Daniel Radcliffe
Condoleezza Rice
Marla Runyan
Ruth Simmons
Mattie Stepanek
J.R.R. Tolkien
Barry Watson
Tyrone Willingham
Elijah Wood

2003

Yolanda Adams
Olivia Bennett
Mildred Benson
Alexis Bledel
Barry Bonds
Vincent Brooks
Laura Bush
Amanda Bynes
Kelly Clarkson
Vin Diesel
Eminem
Michele Forman
Vicente Fox
Millard Fuller
Josh Hartnett
Dolores Huerta
Sarah Hughes
Enrique Iglesias
Jeanette Lee
John Lewis
Nicklas Lidstrom
Clint Mathis
Donovan McNabb
Nelly
Andy Roddick
Gwen Stefani
Emma Watson
Meg Whitman
Reese Witherspoon
Yao Ming

Biography Today

Subject Series

Expands and complements the General Series and targets specific subject areas . . .

Our readers asked for it! They wanted more biographies, and the *Biography Today* **Subject Series** is our response to that demand. Now your readers can choose their special areas of interest and go on to read about their favorites in those fields. Priced at just $39 per volume, the following specific volumes are included in the *Biography Today* **Subject Series:**

- **Artists**
- **Authors**
- **Performing Artists**
- **Scientists & Inventors**
- **Sports**
- **World Leaders**
  Environmental Leaders
  Modern African Leaders

AUTHORS

"A useful tool for children's assignment needs." — *School Library Journal*

"The prose is workmanlike: report writers will find enough detail to begin sound investigations, and browsers are likely to find someone of interest." — *School Library Journal*

SCIENTISTS & INVENTORS

"The articles are readable, attractively laid out, and touch on important points that will suit assignment needs. Browsers will note the clear writing and interesting details." — *School Library Journal*

"The book is excellent for demonstrating that scientists are real people with widely diverse backgrounds and personal interests. The biographies are fascinating to read." — *The Science Teacher*

SPORTS

"This series should become a standard resource in libraries that serve intermediate students." — *School Library Journal*

ENVIRONMENTAL LEADERS #1

"A tremendous book that fills a gap in the biographical category of books. This is a great reference book." — *Science Scope*

FEATURES AND FORMAT

- Sturdy 6" x 9" hardbound volumes
- Individual volumes, $39 each
- 200 pages per volume
- 10-12 profiles per volume — targets individuals within a specific subject area
- Contact sources for additional information
- Cumulative General, Places of Birth, and Birthday Indexes

NOTE: There is *no duplication of entries* between the **General Series** of *Biography Today* and the **Subject Series**.

Artists

VOLUME 1

Ansel Adams
Romare Bearden
Margaret Bourke-White
Alexander Calder
Marc Chagall
Helen Frankenthaler
Jasper Johns
Jacob Lawrence
Henry Moore
Grandma Moses
Louise Nevelson
Georgia O'Keeffe
Gordon Parks
I.M. Pei
Diego Rivera
Norman Rockwell
Andy Warhol
Frank Lloyd Wright

Authors

VOLUME 1

Eric Carle
Alice Childress
Robert Cormier
Roald Dahl
Jim Davis
John Grisham
Virginia Hamilton
James Herriot
S.E. Hinton
M.E. Kerr
Stephen King
Gary Larson
Joan Lowery Nixon
Gary Paulsen
Cynthia Rylant
Mildred D. Taylor
Kurt Vonnegut, Jr.
E.B. White
Paul Zindel

VOLUME 2

James Baldwin
Stan and Jan Berenstain
David Macaulay
Patricia MacLachlan
Scott O'Dell
Jerry Pinkney
Jack Prelutsky

Lynn Reid Banks
Faith Ringgold
J.D. Salinger
Charles Schulz
Maurice Sendak
P.L. Travers
Garth Williams

VOLUME 3

Candy Dawson Boyd
Ray Bradbury
Gwendolyn Brooks
Ralph W. Ellison
Louise Fitzhugh
Jean Craighead George
E.L. Konigsburg
C.S. Lewis
Fredrick L. McKissack
Patricia C. McKissack
Katherine Paterson
Anne Rice
Shel Silverstein
Laura Ingalls Wilder

VOLUME 4

Betsy Byars
Chris Carter
Caroline B. Cooney
Christopher Paul Curtis
Anne Frank
Robert Heinlein
Marguerite Henry
Lois Lowry
Melissa Mathison
Bill Peet
August Wilson

VOLUME 5

Sharon Creech
Michael Crichton
Karen Cushman
Tomie dePaola
Lorraine Hansberry
Karen Hesse
Brian Jacques
Gary Soto
Richard Wright
Laurence Yep

VOLUME 6

Lloyd Alexander
Paula Danziger
Nancy Farmer
Zora Neale Hurston

Shirley Jackson
Angela Johnson
Jon Krakauer
Leo Lionni
Francine Pascal
Louis Sachar
Kevin Williamson

VOLUME 7

William H. Armstrong
Patricia Reilly Giff
Langston Hughes
Stan Lee
Julius Lester
Robert Pinsky
Todd Strasser
Jacqueline Woodson
Patricia C. Wrede
Jane Yolen

VOLUME 8

Amelia Atwater-Rhodes
Barbara Cooney
Paul Laurence Dunbar
Ursula K. Le Guin
Farley Mowat
Naomi Shihab Nye
Daniel Pinkwater
Beatrix Potter
Ann Rinaldi

VOLUME 9

Robb Armstrong
Cherie Bennett
Bruce Coville
Rosa Guy
Harper Lee
Irene Gut Opdyke
Philip Pullman
Jon Scieszka
Amy Tan
Joss Whedon

VOLUME 10

David Almond
Joan Bauer
Kate DiCamillo
Jack Gantos
Aaron McGruder
Richard Peck
Andrea Davis Pinkney
Louise Rennison
David Small
Katie Tarbox

VOLUME 11

Laurie Halse Anderson
Bryan Collier
Margaret Peterson
  Haddix
Milton Meltzer
William Sleator
Sonya Sones
Genndy Tartakovsky
Wendelin Van Draanen
Ruth White

VOLUME 12

An Na
Claude Brown
Meg Cabot
Virginia Hamilton
Chuck Jones
Robert Lipsyte
Lillian Morrison
Linda Sue Park
Pam Muñoz Ryan
Lemony Snicket
  (Daniel Handler)

VOLUME 13

Andrew Clements
Eoin Colfer
Sharon Flake
Edward Gorey
Francisco Jiménez
Astrid Lindgren
Chris Lynch
Marilyn Nelson
Tamora Pierce
Virginia Euwer Wolff

Performing Artists

VOLUME 1

Jackie Chan
Dixie Chicks
Kirsten Dunst
Suzanne Farrell
Bernie Mac
Shakira
Isaac Stern
Julie Taymor
Usher
Christina Vidal

VOLUME 2

Ashanti
Tyra Banks
Peter Jackson
Norah Jones
Quincy Jones
Avril Lavigne
George López
Marcel Marceau
Eddie Murphy
Julia Stiles

Scientists & Inventors

VOLUME 1

John Bardeen
Sylvia Earle
Dian Fossey
Jane Goodall
Bernadine Healy
Jack Horner
Mathilde Krim
Edwin Land
Louise & Mary Leakey
Rita Levi-Montalcini
J. Robert Oppenheimer
Albert Sabin
Carl Sagan
James D. Watson

VOLUME 2

Jane Brody
Seymour Cray
Paul Erdös
Walter Gilbert
Stephen Jay Gould
Shirley Ann Jackson
Raymond Kurzweil
Shannon Lucid
Margaret Mead
Garrett Morgan
Bill Nye
Eloy Rodriguez
An Wang

VOLUME 3

Luis W. Alvarez
Hans A. Bethe
Gro Harlem Brundtland
Mary S. Calderone
Ioana Dumitriu

Temple Grandin
John Langston
  Gwaltney
Bernard Harris
Jerome Lemelson
Susan Love
Ruth Patrick
Oliver Sacks
Richie Stachowski

VOLUME 4

David Attenborough
Robert Ballard
Ben Carson
Eileen Collins
Biruté Galdikas
Lonnie Johnson
Meg Lowman
Forrest Mars Sr.
Akio Morita
Janese Swanson

VOLUME 5

Steve Case
Douglas Engelbart
Shawn Fanning
Sarah Flannery
Bill Gates
Laura Groppe
Grace Murray Hopper
Steven Jobs
Rand and Robyn Miller
Shigeru Miyamoto
Steve Wozniak

VOLUME 6

Hazel Barton
Alexa Canady
Arthur Caplan
Francis Collins
Gertrude Elion
Henry Heimlich
David Ho
Kenneth Kamler
Lucy Spelman
Lydia Villa-Komaroff

VOLUME 7

Tim Berners-Lee
France Córdova
Anthony S. Fauci
Sue Hendrickson
Steve Irwin
John Forbes Nash, Jr.

Jerri Nielsen
Ryan Patterson
Nina Vasan
Gloria WilderBrathwaite

VOLUME 8

Deborah Blum
Richard Carmona
Helene Gayle
Dave Kapell
Adriana C. Ocampo
John Romero
Jamie Rubin
Jill Tarter
Earl Warrick
Edward O. Wilson

Sports

VOLUME 1

Hank Aaron
Kareem Abdul-Jabbar
Hassiba Boulmerka
Susan Butcher
Beth Daniel
Chris Evert
Ken Griffey, Jr.
Florence Griffith Joyner
Grant Hill
Greg LeMond
Pelé
Uta Pippig
Cal Ripken, Jr.
Arantxa Sanchez Vicario
Deion Sanders
Tiger Woods

VOLUME 2

Muhammad Ali
Donovan Bailey
Gail Devers
John Elway
Brett Favre
Mia Hamm
Anfernee "Penny"
  Hardaway
Martina Hingis
Gordie Howe
Jack Nicklaus
Richard Petty
Dot Richardson
Sheryl Swoopes
Steve Yzerman

VOLUME 3

Joe Dumars
Jim Harbaugh
Dominik Hasek
Michelle Kwan
Rebecca Lobo
Greg Maddux
Fatuma Roba
Jackie Robinson
John Stockton
Picabo Street
Pat Summitt
Amy Van Dyken

VOLUME 4

Wilt Chamberlain
Brandi Chastain
Derek Jeter
Karch Kiraly
Alex Lowe
Randy Moss
Se Ri Pak
Dawn Riley
Karen Smyers
Kurt Warner
Serena Williams

VOLUME 5

Vince Carter
Lindsay Davenport
Lisa Fernandez
Fu Mingxia
Jaromir Jagr
Marion Jones
Pedro Martinez
Warren Sapp
Jenny Thompson
Karrie Webb

VOLUME 6

Jennifer Capriati
Stacy Dragila
Kevin Garnett
Eddie George
Alex Rodriguez
Joe Sakic
Annika Sorenstam
Jackie Stiles
Tiger Woods
Aliy Zirkle

VOLUME 7

Tom Brady
Tara Dakides
Alison Dunlap
Sergio Garcia

Allen Iverson
Shirley Muldowney
Ty Murray
Patrick Roy
Tasha Schwiker

VOLUME 8

Simon Ammann
Shannon Bahrke
Kelly Clark
Vonetta Flowers
Cammi Granato
Chris Klug
Jonny Moseley
Apolo Ohno
Sylke Otto
Ryne Sanborn
Jim Shea, Jr.

VOLUME 9

Tori Allen
Layne Beachley
Sue Bird
Fabiola da Silva
Randy Johnson
Jason Kidd
Tony Stewart
Michael Vick
Ted Williams
Jay Yelas

World Leaders

VOLUME 1: Environmental Leaders 1

Edward Abbey
Renee Askins
David Brower
Rachel Carson
Marjory Stoneman
   Douglas
Dave Foreman
Lois Gibbs
Wangari Maathai
Chico Mendes
Russell A. Mittermeier
Margaret and Olaus J.
   Murie
Patsy Ruth Oliver
Roger Tory Peterson

Ken Saro-Wiwa
Paul Watson
Adam Werbach

VOLUME 2: Modern African Leaders

Mohammed Farah
   Aidid
Idi Amin
Hastings Kamuzu Banda
Haile Selassie
Hassan II
Kenneth Kaunda
Jomo Kenyatta
Winnie Mandela
Mobutu Sese Seko
Robert Mugabe
Kwame Nkrumah
Julius Kambarage
   Nyerere
Anwar Sadat
Jonas Savimbi
Léopold Sédar Senghor
William V. S. Tubman

VOLUME 3: Environmental Leaders 2

John Cronin
Dai Qing
Ka Hsaw Wa
Winona LaDuke
Aldo Leopold
Bernard Martin
Cynthia Moss
John Muir
Gaylord Nelson
Douglas Tompkins
Hazel Wolf